D0150108

Healing
the Pain of
Everyday
Loss

Healing the Pain of Everyday Loss

by Ira J. Tanner

Winston Press

Front cover photo: Cyril A. Reilly

Copyright © 1976 by Ira J. Tanner. Copyright under International
and Pan-American Copyright Conventions. Published by arrangement
with Hawthorn Books, a division of Elsevier-Dutton Publishing Co.,
Inc. All rights reserved.

Library of Congress Catalog Card Number: 80-51112
ISBN: 0-03-057849-3
Printed in the United States of America.

Winston Press, Inc.
430 Oak Grove
Minneapolis, Minnesota 55403

5 4 3 2

For June

Contents

Healing
the Pain of
Everyday
Loss

Introduction

This is not just a book on death and dying; from the start I want to make that clear. I shall deal with the subject of change and the ten broad categories of ordinary loss in everyday life and, for the sake of robust emotional and physical health, why we must thoroughly grieve any loss.

Grief, to my mind, is our reaction to any loss. Our chronicle of losses is, of course, inexhaustible—beyond calculation. Each day we grieve the loss of *something, someone,* or *some place* important to us. Here is Jim, for instance, who has bought a new car. He likes all of its fancy new features, among them an FM radio and electric windows, but he also grieves the loss of the old car, an eight-year-old model. The family took it on several memorable vacations and, as with anything that serves us well, they grew to trust its dependability and became attached to it. We grieve the loss of any object in which we have invested not only our money but our time and affection as well. Jim and his family "loved" that old car and it is perfectly normal that they grieve its loss.

Yet, we continue to reserve the word *grief* and the grieving process itself for one massive loss in our lives: death. But even then we feel awkward and embarrassed, as if grieving is unhealthy, or worse—abnormal.

Why do we persist in clinging to this galvanized belief? Is death our only loss in life? Of course not. In fact, the lion's share of grief does not surround the death of a person at all. The loss of any material goods or the failure to reach a longed-for goal are the common occasions for grieving. We grieve these losses because they represent the loss of our chosen life-style.

That all forms of loss embrace feelings and stages in common first came to me in the early days of my counseling practice. I saw that someone grieving retirement or divorce went through the same stages of grief as someone grieving the death of a loved one. And, often, patients said they grieved a broken friendship harder than had the friend actually died. In sum, comparing grief patterns I discovered that although stages of grief were not identical in number or order, the similarities were startling. (I will expand on them in chapter 6.)

It Can't Happen to Me

Many of us are caught up in the false notion that major losses, such as blindness, a car crash, or even death itself, are reserved for others and not for us. Somehow we convince ourselves that we will always be spared. Dr. William Nesbitt, of the University of California Medical School in Sacramento, believes that the reason people gather at the scene of an accident to gawk and mill around in numbed silence is that the fractured bodies and cars confirm the no-

4

tion that the worst losses in life do *indeed* strike others. "Isn't this accident horrible?" they whisper to each other, simultaneously feeling satisfaction that their notion has been confirmed.

This attitude is in one sense healthy. Who wants to dwell upon morbid possibilities? But even if we could conceive that "I" am a potential victim of any loss, our minds cannot grasp the full magnitude of what it would be like to go blind or lose a leg.

Loss as Personal Defeat

We cannot control everything that happens to us but we *are* responsible for our reaction to everything that happens to us. We need goals, but we have to leave room for change and loss.

Consider the notion of loss as personal defeat. I think of Marilyn, public relations director for a hosiery firm. Company policy requires all employees to retire no later than age sixty-five. But Marilyn was retired at age sixty-two, as part of a shift in personnel. "I was livid," she recalls. "I took that change as a personal defeat for it was out of my hands." If we, like Marilyn, believe we have power to control the outcome of events and commitments, we then grieve the loss of our power if events don't unfold as we planned.

Money Compensates for Loss

Another misconception we hold about loss is that life and objects have monetary value entitling us to money upon their departure. Pianists insure their hands, opera stars their voices, and athletes their bodies. We insure everything from diamond rings to automobiles to human life. Monetary compensation eases the sting of loss. We have something to show for loss, some tangible evidence of the worth of the loss. Sitting on a shelf in my home is a tiny wooden sled made by my father when he was nine years old, which mother gave me shortly after his death. It consists of three pieces of wood nailed together, so the material isn't worth anything. I cannot place a monetary value on it, however, because it represents my father's youth and it is priceless to me.

The Language of Grief

No amount of money, of course, can begin to compensate for the loss of a love. Similarly, no word or combination of words fully expresses our grief feelings. Words are only marks on paper that do not convey the quality or force of our feelings, our fantasies, or our loneliness.

Even the most eloquent of words cannot describe our grief feelings. C. S. Lewis writes: "Grief feels most like fear. No one ever told me loss felt like fear. The fluttering in my stomach, the same yawning, and I keep swallowing. Perhaps, more strictly, it feels like suspense. Or like waiting, just hanging about waiting for something to happen. I can't settle down. I fidget. I smoke too much. Up until this loss I had too little time. Now there is nothing but time."[1]

1. C. S. Lewis, *A Grief Observed* (New York: Seabury Press, 1961), p. 7.

With Colin Murray Parker grieving closely resembles a physical injury: "The loss may be spoken of as a blow. As in the case of a physical injury, the 'wound' heals gradually. But occasionally complications set in, healing is delayed, or a further injury reopens a healing wound."[2]

Edgar N. Jackson simply writes: "Grief is a universal human experience. It is the strong emotion we feel when we come face to face with the death of someone who has been a part of our lives."[3]

Any written or verbal definition of an emotion, I believe, falls short. Just as a painting is a blending of many separate colors, life is a blending of many moods and feelings: fun, loneliness, love, for example. Yet one is not disconnected from the other with a clear beginning or an abrupt ending. Needing to express grief we feel such a desert inside, a poverty, that the deepest and truest things about our feelings will stay unsaid, stretching beyond words. And the more deeply we grieve the larger our agony of nonexpression. Words grow fewer. Finally there are none. Feeling deeply the exhaustion of words, not their eloquence, is testimony of the quality of our feelings. Touching or being touched "says" more than words. From childhood a touch is the most comforting mode of communication.

Our Search for Solutions

It would be wonderful if we could come up with an absolute solution, like touching, to soothe the griever. But un-

2. Colin Murray Parker, *Bereavement, Studies of Grief in Adult Life* (New York: International Studies Press, 1972), p. 5.

3. Edgar J. Jackson, *You and Your Grief* (New York: Channel Press, 1961), p. 11.

fortunately there are no simple solutions, only intelligent choices. Each choice is a risk, for its outcome cannot be predicted.

Experts promising a solution to sexual dysfunction, obesity, loneliness, or grief mislead us. When Dr. Atkins promises that his high-protein diet is a cure-all for obesity, or Dr. Reuben touts his *Save Your Life Diet* as the diet to end all diets, people sit up and take notice. We're ecstatic whenever someone promises a method for eliminating overweight and obesity. But those of us who doggedly pursue solutions, going from diet to diet, doctor to doctor, book to book, end up frustrated and disappointed. We live in the delusion that "maybe next time" we will find the final answer. But no form of human suffering can be eliminated with absolute certainty. If life held solutions, what worked for you would work for everyone and forever. But it doesn't. We are unique persons and we are changing daily.

Today's choices are meant to meet only today's needs. We have to choose with the knowledge that choices do not permanently eliminate our obstacle but assist us through it in such fashion as to derive maximum benefit from the struggle itself. Most people find that the best way around a problem is to go through it.

One area in which we seek simple solutions is child-raising. Parenthood would be perennially delightful if the solutions presented in child-raising books worked for everyone and every time. Some parents go to page such-and-such looking for the solution each time their child misbehaves. But parents need to trust their judgment too, and realize that their children are changing and so are they. Even the baby expert himself, Dr. Benjamin Spock, periodically updates the ideas presented in his first baby book.

There are guidelines for child-raising—yes, but guidelines are not absolutes. Every rule has an exception. A parent sensitive to the moods and needs of children knows that sending misbehaving children to their room is not always the solution. Sometimes a misbehaving child is indirectly pleading for love. One ten-year-old boy told me the only way he could ever get his father's attention was to pick a fight with his brother. That way his father noticed him, even if the attention was a reprimand and an occasional swat. Such attention, the young fellow said, was better than none at all.

A woman client once asked me for an absolute answer to the question "Will I ever get this depressed again?" I would have liked to give her the absolute assurance, "No." Instead I said, "You *need* not but I cannot give you a guarantee that you *will* not."

There is no absolute way to work through grief following the loss of any love. This is a book on choices you can make while grieving not just to help you endure grief, but to help you emerge from grief a wiser, more sensitive, and more aware person.

Part I
What Is Loss?

1
The Scope of Loss

Loss—what is it? What is it not?

Consider these losses. Jan, for example, a woman of thirty-one: "Just look at my figure, I'm nothing but a fat slob," she sobs softly, the fanned fingers of one hand covering her face. Once she was full of confidence and reigned over a county fair as beauty queen. Today, swollen by compulsive eating, she is angry "for letting myself get this fat," guilty "because I can never say no to food." Someone slim is apt to scoff at grief like that, not understanding that compulsive eaters often feel helpless to stop eating.

Or listen to Jim, who, after smoking cigarettes for thirty-five years, decides to quit. All those years smoking has been a relaxing ritual for him. Feeling tense at work he lit a cigarette to "unwind." After meals, smoking was especially pleasurable. When he felt ill at ease at a party, the smoking ritual helped him to relax while conversing. Giving up this habit is a severe loss. "Ridiculous," quips a nonsmoker sarcastically, "Jim should be glad he has the common sense to quit." But smoking is an addiction. Therefore quitting is much more than throwing away what remains of a carton of cigarettes. It is finding a substitute for the ritual itself and slowly conquering nicotine addiction.

Then consider Helen, who upon entering the church on Sunday morning finds someone occupying her favorite seat in her favorite pew. Over twenty-five years Helen has gravitated to that same spot. Its loss, this Sunday, hilarious to one hearing her tell it over coffee after church, is one Helen grieves all of Sunday.

What we consider to be "loss" others are apt to brand as gain; or they may scoff at our loss—even find it humorous. Don Rickles has made a fortune poking fun at the losses and misfortunes of people in his audience. Not many of us are able to get by with that. Feelings of loss are delicate. Sharing these feelings with someone is a gift of the highest order.

When the child grieves the cancellation of a picnic, the well-meaning parent may treat it lightly and thus deprive the child of his grief feelings. Clearly we do not see eye to eye on what constitutes "loss," but we should always attempt to understand *feelings of loss* in others.

Feelings of loss flow out of our reaction to change. If time stood still and we did not change physically, emotionally, and mentally each day, and if things did not change for us, we would not grieve. There would be no loss.

Some change, of course, we choose—enlisting in the Peace Corps, marriage. But most change we do not choose, such as the aging process itself or loss of hearing. Regardless of our wishes or best-laid plans, change comes.

Change has two parts: loss and gain. Our central point is, until after a change has occurred we do not know whether it will be construed as net loss or net gain. Parents feel differently about their children marrying. We have all heard the old saying, "You have not lost a son, you have gained a daughter." The bride's parents may feel they have not lost a daughter but gained a son.

When Grief Begins

Feelings of loss begin at birth. The child is thrust from the mother's warm, secure womb and must learn to cope with this loss and adjust to a new environment.

Long before children comprehend the meaning of words, they absorb parents' attitude toward change and observe parents' reactions to ordinary events of the day. Later, equipped with a minivocabulary, children are frequently instructed how they should react to change, what they should feel good or sad about, what they should or should not cry over. Within them conflict arises between how they *do* respond naturally to change and how they should respond to change, as when a favorite toy or blanket is lost or a best friend moves away. They may think, "What reaction will please mommy and daddy most," or, "Will they love me if I cry over this?"

Told "be strong" or "be big" or "what a silly thing to feel bad about," children—out of fear of losing their parents' love—struggle to disown their natural grief reaction.

I do not want to throw a bad light on parents. Rarely do mother and father *intentionally* say or do things to make children feel unloved or unimportant. The problem is the child's position in life; he has no language and can only react to what goes on around him. All in all, somewhere along in the first five years of life, most children decide that grief feelings are appropriate, acceptable, and normal in only one situation: death. Only when a grandparent or a beloved family friend dies does the child see his parents cry and grieve openly.

Sometimes the arrival of a new brother or sister marks a child's first grief experience; he mourns the loss of priority and attention his parents previously bestowed upon him. Later, during puberty, he grieves over his loss of carefree childhood. In girls, this is particularly noticeable with the onset of menstruation.

Around age thirteen, many children begin to lose their abilities to conjure up free-wheeling fantasies. Probably they are imitating their parents and other adults who frequently scoff at the child's fantasies or in some other way make him feel embarrassed or childish. However, other children may seek escape from the adult world by retreating completely into a world of make-believe.

I remember the exact day that my private world of make-believe slipped away from me. It was a cold, brisk March day. I was sitting on the edge of my bed and playing my "drums" in rhythm with the orchestra music that blared over the radio. Then it happened—I opened my eyes and saw in my hands not drumsticks but two of my mother's butter knives. Instead of drums there were three empty oatmeal boxes, their covers on.

Fantasy, in spite of my best efforts, failed me. Near tears, I squeezed my eyes shut once more and tried to reenter my make-believe world—again I would be a drummer in Glenn Miller's dance band. But it was no use. There would be no more cheering crowds, no spotlight narrowing down on me. I knew I would see my magical world again, but it would no longer be through the eyes of a twelve-year-old. There are days still when I'm tired or discouraged that I close my eyes to shut out the real world for a minute or two, but my command of fantasy is lost forever.

I thought that growing up meant putting away "childish" things, like pretending I was a *real* drummer or *real* cowboy. Or making believe I had wings and could fly. Becoming mature meant solving real-life problems "out there," absorbing facts in history books, and learning how to multiply. The rewards of that learning were great, but in the process of understanding reality I lost touch, in part, with childlike fantasy inside myself.

Loss and Personal Values

The changes we grieve as loss reveal the quality of our values. Therefore, one who judges our losses as trivial, or even not as loss, is judging the nature of our values. What we grieve as loss is the truest indicator of our values.

For example, when we tell someone we "feel bad" at the death of a houseplant that has hung in our kitchen for five years, we cannot predict their response. Fond themselves of houseplants and believing their care is not a waste of time or money, they will empathize with our feelings; devoid of interest in plants, their reaction to our loss may be one of bewilderment.

We do not agree on what constitutes a friendship, so sharing our grief over loss of a friend is a high risk. The people we choose for friends, others would never choose. Our values and needs differ. When Janet disclosed her grief to Alice over breaking up with her fiance, Alice responded coldly, "I'd say you're smart, I never could see much good in that man." Such judgments indict our ideals, question our choices, mock our commitments. We do not ask friends to agree with our values, only understand our feelings of loss of a love.

One day while driving through the countryside close to my home, I spotted an eighth grade neighbor boy walking stooped over and dragging a large plastic bag behind him. He was picking up tin cans and bottles along the road. My friend commented, "Hasn't that kid got anything better to do?" The next day I met my young friend and mentioned I had seen him picking up refuse along the road. He answered, "Yeah, I do that about once a month because I feel bad about our messy landscape." This teen-ager was grieving the loss of a clean landscape and, in addition, doing something to correct the loss. A cluttered landscape was evidently not cause for grief in my passenger.

Losses and Gains

Immediately after a loss, feelings cloud our thinking. As feelings soften, however, the clouds begin to lift and thoughts of gain materialize. Unfortunately, we too often feel guilty about the gain.

Typical is the reaction of a woman who feels great loss after enrolling her five-year-old in kindergarten. She felt an emotional separation as strong as the physical separation when her daughter went off to school. Without her daughter around, she felt she had nothing to do. But, after a week of feeling lost, she began to see the possible gains. Now she could linger over her breakfast, have an uninterrupted conversation with her husband, or even pursue her own educational or professional interests. At first, she felt guilty about these "luxuries"; now she understands the wisdom of turning her loss into a gain: She uses her quiet mornings to think and plan, her marriage is revitalized through improved communication, and she spends many pleasant hours working with other adults whose interests coincide with her own.

On balance, as time softens grief, the gain often outweighs the loss. Once I put in a bid on three acres of land—a hillside really. The land was dotted with trees and fronted a lake—a fine site for a new house, I thought. Then the landowner reversed his decision to sell. I grieved that loss as 100 percent loss, an opportunity gone forever. Working through the stages of my grief (shock at his decision not to sell, guilt for not making a higher bid, and anger at his decision not to sell), I began to see the gain that accompanied my loss. There would be no big monthly mortgage payments, no plethora of phone calls to line up a contractor. In a way, these gains comforted me.

Grieving Achievements

While working toward a major goal, most of us imagine the feelings of great relief and achievement that we think we'll feel upon reaching our goal. Then, when the big moment arrives, we're surprised to find that, instead of feeling great, we feel depressed.

This happened to me the day I put the finishing touches on a book I had been writing for two years. Instead of the elation I thought I should feel (that old *should* again), I felt lost and removed from my family and friends. I panicked, and the panic threw my grieving process topsy-turvy. This was the first time I realized that grief is not reserved for death. Finally, I realized that I was grieving the loss of a familiar routine and a goal that had dominated my life for two years.

Some people grieve upon graduation from school. Recently, a friend who had scrimped and scraped to support his family while he went to school was awarded a prestigious degree. We uncorked a bottle of champagne and toasted the family's bright future: a substantial income, a home in the suburbs—it was all theirs now. Later that night, when my friend prepared to go, his spirit seemed heavy.

"What's the matter?" I asked.

"Would you believe," he responded, "that I am grieving the loss of a goal that I scrambled after for eight years." His embarrassment over his grief feelings at a time when we were all celebrating his achievement prompted him to try to hide his feelings and deny his grief.

Grieving a Decision to Marry

"I've had lots of tears lately when I should be feeling happy," a woman client recently confided. "I hate change, especially when things are going so right for me."

Her first marriage had ended in divorce, whereupon she launched a successful career as a buyer for a large department store. Her job took her on business trips around the country; she grew increasingly more independent and confident—a new feeling for her. While she loved her present fiance deeply and wanted to marry him, she also feared that her approaching marriage would cause her to lose her newfound independence. Working through grief feelings in counseling, she came to see the gains she got with her marriage far outweighed the loss of independence she expected. Her husband realized the importance of supporting his wife in her work and has therefore avoided making unreasonable demands on her time.

2
The Process of Healing

Physical and emotional healing require three things: information, validation, and confrontation.

1. *Crystal clear information on the facts of healing.* Recently, over noon lunch, I had a conversation with a woman whose job is explaining all sides of hospitalization and recovery to incoming patients: the treatment process itself, the gradual buildup of exercise, diet, visitation privileges, and how soon the patient can go home. Enlightened patients, she stresses, those who know what to expect, heal quicker than those with little or no information.

Think of grief as a healing process through which the fact of loss—any loss—is "made real" to us. Knowing what feelings to expect—that grieving loss of a pet or friendship is normal, that self-pity is not abnormal, that anger is common—clears up fear and ignorance, allowing the grieving process to flow naturally.

2. *Validation* is required for sound mental and emotional healing. The word *validation* means confirming or "making sure." Informed by the doctor we have a terminal illness with six months to live, we will in all likelihood seek the

validation of a second doctor, even a third. That declaration is too massive for us to comprehend. It may take the validation of several doctors for the news to begin sinking in.

We tend, you see, to be distrustful of our loss feelings, particularly a traumatic loss. We cannot fathom what is happening to us, maybe it isn't happening at all. We need others—their listening, words, sheer presence—to validate our reaction, assure us that yes, the loss has indeed happened, that yes, we can trust our feelings of loss.

Some of the most excruciating grief I have ever witnessed has been on occasions where not death but ordinary events have separated people: loss of a son or daughter to the ravages of drugs, bankruptcy, loss of trust within a vintage relationship. Ann, for instance, upon being told her son was institutionalized for alcoholism, inquired over and over of several close friends, "Is it really true?" To herself she wondered if she was dreaming. But the passing of time coupled with persistent and patient validation helped to gradually make the loss real to her. "It would have been easier," she mourned, "had he actually died."

A funeral helps validate the reality of a death. A woman told me her husband was killed when the small airplane he was piloting crashed into the ocean about one mile offshore. Two survived but three others, her husband included, were killed. Rescuers found every body except her husband's. Said the widow, "If they had recovered his body all doubt of his death would be removed. The plane crashed eighteen months ago, but my mind still continues to play tricks on me. Maybe he's still alive. The loss doesn't seem real yet. It probably never will."

After friends help validate our loss they keep on validating the authenticity of far-ranging feelings during the grieving process itself. You may inquire of a friend, for instance, if your guilt over loss of an opportunity is "normal," or if it is okay to feel angry over loss of a minister, priest, or rabbi who has moved away. The griever needs to hear a friend say that such feelings are to be expected. Why? Because if another values our feelings, we "own" them within ourselves and do not deny the grieving process.

Here is part of a conversation I had with Kay, whose daughter, now three weeks old, was born blind.

> KAY: It's very hard for me to talk about Laurie's blindness. My husband still can't say what he's feeling about it.
> I. T. It must be very hard for you to talk about.
> KAY: We had such high hopes for a normal baby. Ever since the birth I've felt guilty wondering if I did something during the pregnancy to cause Laurie's blindness. I guess I shouldn't feel that way, but . . .
> I. T. Sounds like on the one hand you're feeling guilty and on the other hand wondering if you should feel that way.
> KAY: That's right, though I suppose it's normal to think back like I'm doing and wonder.
> I. T. Feeling guilty after a loss is quite a normal reaction.

Kay not only felt guilty, she felt guilty about feeling guilty and needed someone to validate the authenticity of her guilt, tell her it was "normal" to feel as she did. If she went on denying guilt her grieving process would be slowed.

3. Responsible *confrontation* is also necessary for sound physical and emotional healing. Recovering from an operation, we are apt to grow discouraged or begin chafing under limits the doctor has set on our activities. So we need to be

reminded that our recklessness is taxing the healing process.

The same rule applies to grief. Grief is hard work during which we may grow tired or get stuck in a stage, prompting friends to confront us with our need to get on with grief, even jar us out of self-pity and morbidness. Knowing *when* to confront requires wisdom, skill, and compassion.

The real difference between people lies not in our opportunities but in our abilities to recognize opportunities. Opportunities are everywhere.

The last place many of us look for opportunities is within the grieving process. What good can come of such emotional trauma? We can think of but one challenge: Get grief behind us as quickly as possible. Many of my students and clients say grief is the most traumatic process they have gone through because the loss of someone or something important to them made them aware of *themselves*. We do grieve the actual loss, but in addition we grieve for ourselves, questioning, "What is going to happen to me now?" Loss triggers awareness of dependency needs and requires we scrutinize our goals, values, and talents. If that awareness frightens us, we will escape by keeping ourselves busy, thus denying ourselves the opportunity to tap previously unexplored inner resources, and risk new ventures.

3
Mastering Our Losses through Grief

Today things happen so fast that many of us are locked into perpetual grief, cheated of time between losses in which to thoroughly grieve. Gail, for instance, changed locations ten times, lost her store clerk job, her father died, then her marriage crumbled—all within four years. Grieving continuously, she has been unable to carry on her normal duties for two years.

Perhaps you are one of the American families who changed locations this year. Today, with 80 percent of the population residing on 20 percent of the land, many of us grieve loss of a feeling of community, of belonging, which a nonmetropolitan area offers. We yearn for a main street along which are located all of the stores in town, the restaurant where people gathered to talk of community events. We miss addressing the druggist, postmaster, and doctor by his/her first name and in return being addressed by our first name.

Following a move, returning frequently is one way of working through unresolved grief. If the move was traumatic, we may "go home" often. One such transplant, who moved from the Midwest to California, drove back seven successive summers before his grief softened.

Numerous city transplants grieve loss of contact with nature and the soil, one reason 85 million Americans have taken up gardening and indoor plants as a hobby. Dr. Seymour Gold, assistant professor of environmental planning at the University of California at Davis says:

> No single item could change the physical and social character of urban America more quickly and dramatically and be less controversial and costly than plants.
>
> People are turning their backs on the flashing neon lights, the telephone wires, the blight that breeds tension and anxieties.
>
> In addition, more young couples are choosing not to have children and their plants become their surrogate babies. Also drawing Americans to the soil is "an environmental guilt" for what we've done to our landscape.

Some losses in the wake of "progress" produce a community grief. In the *Sacramento Bee* a rather terse announcement appeared one day that a grocery corporation intended to purchase a majestic old movie palace downtown, tear it down, and build a supermarket. Protest letters from citizens flooded offices of city officials and a Save the Alhambra group was formed to raise money to purchase the theater and save it. But the drive fell short so the theater was razed, and those who loved history and those who loved that building grieved.

Most letters to the editor in newspapers are expressions of grief over changes within the community—a proposed new freeway that will slice through a part of town or the firing of a popular baseball manager, for example.

In Elk Grove, California, a Save the Trees army was mobilized which won a delay preventing the widening of a proposed boulevard and the cutting down of some 100 trees. The town's citizens felt the trees were impossible to replace and provided a good image, offered protection from the wind, and reduced the noise factor. But mainly they were part of the town's culture, and citizens would severely grieve that loss.

On a national level, think of the rapid change within the field of organized religion, the struggle between conservatives who insist on keeping things as they have always been and the liberals who claim the church is out of step with the times. Some people on principle alone resist change, tout tradition as king, insist the "good old days" were the best and most sensible. Protesting new liturgies, updated translations of the Bible, and a new breed of clergyman who risk speaking out on social issues, many have abandoned the organized church or sought membership in a different church. Some have found contentment; others are church jumpers who will never be able to recapture the good old days. Perhaps the sentiment of a portion of today's youth is summed up in the words written on a placard carried by a college student, Jesus yes, Christianity no.

Then our new morality—the "permissive society" in which communal living, the sexual revolution, experimentation with mind-expanding drugs, the free-speech movement, and trial marriages are gaining acceptance—has left large chunks of the population who grieve loss of "morality."

Consider Glasser, Sommerhill, Montessori, and others who have revolutioned the philosophy of education since World War II. Some see gain in these changes; others grieve the changes as loss. And what of the issues of prayer in public schools, forced busing, and federal aid to parochial schools? Grieving parents, balking at change, carry placards, picket and even bomb property. Violence, however, though making headlines in newspapers, has failed to deter the accelerating rate of social change.

But swift change has struck the hardest blow at the family structure (the loss of stability following frequent moves, the advent of television leaving no time in which to communicate, and the mounting divorce rate). The predominant outgrowth of family unrest is loss of trust between family members. Trust is the foundation upon which the family is built, so when trust decays so does everything else. What is the answer to this growing loss of trust? There is no absolute solution. In some instances, families need to spend more time together, but it is the quality and not the quantity of time we spend together that counts. Children do not demand long hours with parents. And husbands and wives who just spend time together do not necessarily stay together. High-quality communication is what's missing.

It is important to know that hearing is not the same as listening. We can hear someone's words without listening to the feelings behind the words. Understanding is on a feeling level, and with understanding comes trust.

Take this thing called progress. Is it gain or loss? Or does it consist of doing nothing at all, as was decided recently by an American-Canadian Commission when they voted not to interfere with the occasional rockslides at Niagara Falls. Resisting the temptation to improve on nature, the commission decided that progress was allowing nature to adjust to change within herself, repairing, filling in on her own timetable.

The good life, journalist Marya Mannes believes, exists only when you stop wanting a better one and of savoring what is rather than longing for what might be. There is the point at which salvation lies in saying what we have will do, what we make of it is up to us.

The acceleration of progress—"Ford has a better idea"—creates discontent within us. We grow restless with our possessions. Whereas prior to an increase in our salary we purchased our clothes off the rack in the store, now we order custom-made suits and dresses. Whereas we once drove an inexpensive automobile, now we motor about in an expensive one. That's progress. We upgrade the quality of the old.

Discontent is the thief of progress, the thief stealing contentment, time, and trust. But we can choose our reaction to the rate of change, choose when to say "enough."

4
Children and Loss

Our reaction to loss in adulthood is grounded in what we perceived to be loss as children and the grieving patterns we established then.

Infants develop trust in the first year of life when they become aware of objects and persons. If an adult hides behind baby's bedroom curtain, the infant perceives it to be actual disappearance: The adult is not hiding; the adult is gone! Reappearance constitutes an act of magic. In fact, "Whenever a parent is out of the room during the first year of baby's life, the baby can think of the parent but cannot maintain their image," says Dr. Marc Kluender, clinical psychologist specializing in the treatment of children. As yet the child lacks the internal emotional system to hold the parental image.

Up until six months the baby cannot distinguish between persons. He does not know the difference between a parent and a neighbor. All that really matters is that someone fulfills his needs. Any loving adult will do. "Stranger anxiety" starts between six and nine months when baby begins to distinguish between faces. Now if a neighbor holds him he may cry or reach out for mother or father. The concept of parent (what a parent *is*, what a parent *does*) is forming in the baby's mind.

Child psychiatrist Erik Erikson says that from fifteen months to three years the infant explores, showing he has a mind and will of his own. M. S. Mahler, a psychiatrist, confirms Erikson's view, adding that by the time the child is three he can visualize himself as separate from his parents and in their absence maintain an image of them. Separation anxiety, which psychiatrist Karen Horney speaks of as the infant's response to the feeling of being isolated and helpless in a potentially hostile world, has its roots in the first three years of life. The infant, explains Erikson, is not born with a fear of abandonment.

> The meaning of abandonment has to be learned. The infant is helpless but he does not at first know himself to be helpless. He needs another person in order to live. The minute anything is done to relieve pain, to bring pleasure (feed, warm, dry, powder), learning begins to take place which changes the entire picture. The infant learns to become dependent upon and to seek mothering behavior.[1]

The child then learns there are experiences other than pain but that he is helpless to change the experience from pain to comfort. Erikson says: "When the mothering one is present he has now learned to anticipate the meeting of his

1. Erik Erikson, *Childhood and Society* (New York: W. W. Norton, Inc., 1963), p. 97.

needs. When the mother is not present his needs are frustrated and pain and discomfort are felt. There is the learned interpretation that the absence of the mothering one is a threat to his well-being."[2]

Separation anxiety, regardless of our age, is a part of grief. Since the self is made up of a series of emotional investments in people, places, and pets, the destruction or removal of any of them is experienced as the destruction of a part of one's own selfhood and we feel anxiety.

One such temporary separation for children is hospitalization. Children's grief reaction to hospitalization may be crying, screaming, clinging to parents, eating or sleeping poorly, resisting medication. The toddler, still too young in development to grasp the meaning of the separation, can express his needs only in a primitive manner. The older child is better able to understand what going to the hospital means. In either case, however, young children who are not given reasons for hospitalization may conclude they are being punished or sent away forever because they have misbehaved.

Most children from two to fourteen believe their illness is punishment for "bad" behavior or that someone else caused them to fall sick.

The hospitalized preschool child, acutely anxious upon departing from mother, will seek to recapture her by shaking his cot or wailing loudly, thinking his behavior will bring mother back. Wanting only mother, the child often rejects the caring and services of hospital employees, although clinging to a nurse may occur.

2. Ibid., p. 98.

There are ways to comfort the grieving hospitalized child, one being to give the hospital room a homey feeling with soft rugs, chairs, tables, television set and wall pictures.

Another way to offer comfort is regular parental visitation with the caution that overanxious adults may cause problems for the child. Many doctors like to have mother or father present during stressful times for the child.

Adoption is another cause of grief in children. Parents frequently ask how they should tell the adopted child he/she is adopted. One mother called me on the phone and said, "I'm worried sick. How can I tell Greg the awful truth that we adopted him when he was ten days old." In this case the problem was not how to tell Greg he was adopted but to change the mother's attitude toward adoption, to convince her that adoption was a joyful occasion, not a shameful secret.

We began by discussing birth and that while some children come into the family through the natural event of birth, an adopted child is selected. The adopted child, I told her, is different in an exciting way. If Greg senses his mother's confidence and excitement as she relates the story, he will be glad he is adopted.

When they are giving children information on any subject—sex, particularly—parents' attitudes are always more important than anything parents say.

In this matter of telling a child he is adopted, one thing is certain: If parents do not tell him, some relative, friend, or enemy will let it slip out, producing shock, resentment, and anxiety within the child. The sooner parents tell him, the better.

Is there a "best" age to tell a child he is adopted? A good

time is when he first asks, "Where did I come from?"—remembering that it is not wise to tell the whole story all at once. On such a complex subject, a child is able to absorb only a little information at a time. So a good answer to his first inquiry is, "You grew in a mommy's tummy." Notice the a—"a mommy's tummy." This response may prompt a later inquiry, "Whose tummy did I grow in?" This is a good time to say that some babies live with parents who produced them, other babies live with parents who selected them. What children must know is that either is a good way, and our joyful attitude will be the singular thing to convince them.

We should not be surprised if at first children do not believe what we tell them. Parents should not be upset by this. Children's understanding comes gradually. Nine is an age when much that was not comprehended before is often easily grasped.

If, during childhood, physical separations are frequent, some children are inflicted with damaging loss of trust in parents. Take divorce as an example. A child of four cannot comprehend why his mother and father are divorcing. Perhaps the reason is *him*, that he is no longer lovable or that something he has done caused the breakup.

Chief among childhood losses is love. Sometimes the loss of love is a *fact* when the parents do not give the love required to meet a child's needs. Usually, however, a child misinterprets parents' lack of response to mean he is not lovable or that parents do not love him. Father may not notice that two-year-old Jeffrey is reaching up to be held. Mother, talking on the telephone, doesn't hear Jeffrey cry for attention. But Jeffrey, unable to understand, concludes that no response means parents don't care. He grieves that "lack" as loss.

Is it possible to give a child too much love? I have never seen an overloved child; a spoiled child, yes, one sheltered from assuming responsibility. But hugged or rocked too much? Never. Children cannot receive too much love or love given to them for no reason other than that they exist.

Conditional love is given to children as reward for behavior that meets parents' standards. Parents' praise focuses on a child's personality with value judgments like wonderful, dependable, or stupid and hopeless. All are value judgments of a child's character. To a child, *dependable* is as frightening as *stupid*. Either way the child feels that to win parents' love and approval his behavior must meet parents' standards of good behavior. The rule is: Praise a child's effort and achievements, never character. Behavior can be changed but character cannot.

Here is an example of destructive parental praise: "You are such a good kid, Terry, I can always trust you to clean up your room."

Compare that parental statement with this one: "I like the way your room looks, Terry."

This reaction focuses on Terry's effort, leaving his character untouched.

When a second child is born into the family, the first child may grieve the loss of first place, showing his grief through anger; he hits the baby, shuns him, or throws things. Grieving children must know that parents value their anger. Parents can best show they value anger by being permissive with the child's feelings but not with his behavior. A child must know that regardless of how angry he becomes there are definite limits for expressing anger and that if he exceeds the limits he will be punished.

Some good rules for limits in expressing anger are:

1. A child cannot hit mother or father.
2. A child cannot hit a brother or sister.
3. A child cannot call parents or siblings names.
4. A child cannot assault character.
5. A child cannot damage furniture in acting out his anger.

These anger limits give a child permission to release anger in ways unharmful to himself or others. Constructive ways may be pounding the mattress, going somewhere to scream, swimming forty laps in the pool, hitting a punching bag. Any sport requiring contact is excellent for anger expression.

Helping Children through Loss

Children's first questions are about loss. For years "blankie . . . blankie" was a familiar cry in our home. Each of our daughters had a favorite blanket, dragging it everywhere, wearing it down to a shred. Blankie provided comfort and security. If blankie was left behind in the car or under a chair, grief lingered until someone found it.

Here are some firm guidelines for handling children's loss questions.

1. *Answer questions briefly.* It is wise to answer briefly such loss questions as why does daddy (or mommy) leave the house every morning? Why are you moving my

bedroom to a different room? Do you love mommy more than you love me? Never discount a question with "later." A brief response can be accompanied by a reassuring hug or touch. Be truthful without going into detail. Children are intuitive, they know when parents are beating around the bush. Honest answers build trust.

During the first five years of life, a child faces situations which make it necessary for him to bring up questions about death. Parents dread death questions the most. Why? Sometimes we do not have the information to give them, but in addition many parents have not faced the reality of their own impending death and do not want to think or talk about this loss or any loss.

When does a child begin to comprehend the meaning of death?

At the age of three, children start to probe into the origins of death by showing an interest in babies, wondering where baby lived before he was born.

At four, an awareness of life origins has heightened. A child may now conclude that babies can be bought in a department store or that baby comes out through mother's navel or "bottom."

At age five, many children begin to comprehend that death is the end of life. They show distaste for the end by avoiding dead birds and animals lying in the street. This is also the normal age for children to think that people who die can come back to life again.

When age six comes, a child is apt to become emotional about death and when provoked to anger will threaten, "I'm going to kill you." As yet, however, death is something that happens to old people.

By seven, children's perception of death has grown quite clear, and they show curiosity as to the causes of death. In addition children have their first inkling that "I" may die, prompting denial or calm assurance. Disgust with self or the unfairness of others is frequently voiced in the statement, "I wish I were dead," a shocking declaration but one that parents should not take too seriously.

Around eight years, children show interest in what happens after the funeral. Children think heaven is the place you'll go if you're good and hell is the place you'll go if you're bad.

What of children and funerals? If they are curious there is no reason why children should not be allowed to visit the funeral home or attend the funeral itself. But children should not be forced to go. Respect their wishes. Hysterical parents at a funeral frighten children. Other than that, a child attending a funeral will ask new questions about death and life. Most beneficial, however, is that a child feels part of a drama being shared by everyone else in the family. His relationship with family members will be cemented through the common sharing of tears, silence, and touching. If excluded from the funeral, a child will feel cheated and wonder if death is an unnatural loss separate from everyday life.

Grandparents occupy a warm spot in the hearts of grandchildren. One day twelve-year-old Phyllis found a letter on the kitchen counter stating that grandmother had been admitted to a mental hospital. Needing information on mental hospitals and the reason grandmother needed to be in one, Phyllis asked mother to explain. Instead, mother reprimanded Phyllis for reading the letter, ending the conversation with, "When you are old enough to understand, I will explain it to you." A short explanation would have drawn mother and daughter closer together. As it ended, mother squelched this marvelous opportunity, leaving Phyllis anxious and resentful of mother's evasiveness.

Every once in a while children come up with questions such as, "Is Grandma sitting up in the ground?" A brief explanation—"The family wanted to make sure Grandma is comfortable so she is lying down"—is best. Again, no lengthy explanations, just a brief truthful explanation accompanied by a touch or hug.

2. *Recognize all loss feelings.* "You're feeling angry about your goldfish dying aren't you, Johnny?" "I can understand why you would cry after failing your spelling test, Kim."

A parent is not always able or willing to comprehend the magnitude of a child's loss. I think now of Mike, a first grader, who from his bedroom window could observe a family of robins living in a nest in the bushes. One day, as Mike looked on, the family cat sprang onto the nest, devouring the baby birds except for one which fell gravely wounded to the ground. Bolting to the scene, Mike tenderly cupped the baby bird in the palm of his hand, watched it grow limp then die. Helpful parents perceived this to be a devastating loss for Mike, and they responded to his feelings with *reflective listening*, which not only hears children's loss words but understands children's loss feelings.

Here is a positive response to Mike.

MIKE: I'm so mad at the cat for killing the baby bird I'm going to get the ax and cut off his head.

FATHER: You're really angry aren't you Mike? I can understand why you would be angry, but I'm against killing the cat.

Father paraphrased back Mike's feeling, assuring Mike his feeling was understood. In addition, father said he was against killing the cat without lecturing Mike on the "evil" of retaliation.

Contrast the foregoing conversation with this one:

MIKE: Dad, I'm so mad at the cat I'm going to get the ax and cut off his head.

FATHER: The poor cat doesn't understand that killing birds isn't nice, Mike. And how can you say you want to cut his head off?

The unhealthy thing about this response is that father has completely discounted Mike's anger and, in addition, has attempted to make him feel guilty for saying what he did. In all likelihood the conversation ended after father's response. A child's loss feeling may seem dumb, even bizarre, to a parent, but reflective listening refrains from judging feelings.

Mike's parents did not try to cheer him up by taking him to a movie or urge him to "snap out of it." Father helped him to dig a grave alongside the garden, and they even prayed out loud together as Mike laid the bird in the ground in an empty milk carton.

Mike's parents encouraged him to keep doing his normal activities but respected his right to grieve, listening to his feelings and answering questions that came up, like "Why do animals have to kill each other?" For Mike and his entire family, the death of that baby bird was a rich learning experience.

A child who is not permitted to show feelings of grief over the loss of something or someone important to him has no choice other than to fall back on more primitive measures of defense, most often the denial of the pain of loss. If we deny a child the right to grieve, his emotional life grows impoverished. He learns not to feel. He learns not to ask questions, not to think. Children, like adults, have a right to grieve without apology or shame.

Why then do grown-ups rush children through grief? Obviously, it is for the grown-ups' sake.

Observing children grieve gives *us* pain, makes *us* hurt. We are afraid something terrible will happen to their minds. We feel they should always be happy, so our natural instinct is to spare them all of the grief we can. But giving children sufficient time in which to work through grief is a gift, teaching them that whenever they commit themselves to someone or something they will someday feel loss.

Paul Tournier reminds us that all in life is not of equal value. We must learn that, beginning in childhood, "the riches of life lie in those decisive moments when one's life was turned in a new direction. In every life there are a few special moments that count for more than all the rest because they meant the taking of a stand, a self-commitment, a decisive choice. It is commitment that creates the person."[3]

3. Paul Tournier, *The Seasons of Life* (Richmond: John Knox Press, 1961), p. 58.

Whenever we commit ourselves to a person, we know that one day the relationship will end in suffering. Our friend, or we, will move away or die. Or there may be a falling out between us. All love does eventually end in the grief of separation. If our grief following separation is intense, we may choose to not risk a future commitment to someone new. What if that commitment ends in loss too? But then we remain lonely.

3. *Don't make children feel responsible for their losses* Have you ever heard a parent blame children for their loss of fun?

"How can we afford to go anywhere when we have all of you kids to feed?" Or blame children for their loss of health: "Who wouldn't be a nervous wreck with you kids fighting all the time." Or blame children for a divorce: "You didn't help by always taking mother's side." Or death: "You drove your mother to an early grave."

Granted. Children do things to upset parents. They knock over a glass of milk during dinner. They leave socks under the coffee table. They stay on the telephone too long. Parents, like anyone else, are permitted to react to children's behavior. And children need to know what it is about their behavior that aggravates parents. If a parent can say, "I am really mad because you broke the 12:00 midnight curfew," a child listens. But if parents castigate with "You just can't ever be trusted, you stupid idiot," children will get even for the assault on their character by staying out even later next time.

If parents blame children for their reactions, especially loss feelings, children feel responsible for "making it up" to parents by assuming added responsibilities around the house or withholding their feelings from parents in order not to upset them.

Parents need to react to children without blaming them. Here is an example of blame:

"Tom, you make me so mad." If Tom is blamed for anger he will get defensive and then all hope of constructive communication is gone.

But consider this example of reacting:

"I am very angry Tom." We are stating our reaction to Tom without blaming him for our reaction.

In a situation I am thinking of, in a family composed of five daughters and the parents, Alison, the second oldest daughter, senses mother's loss of fun. Alison feels responsible for mother's loss, although she has no reason for feeling that way. Mother is a perfectionist and has chosen to invest all her waking hours satisfying family members' needs. She is choosing to ignore her fun needs and has grown sullen. Alison, to cheer mother up, assumes tasks around the house that the other girls should share in. The point is, Alison is feeling guilty over a problem that is not hers, but mother's.

A crushing grief carried by many parents is children who "turn out wrong." Sharon's parents have always insisted they select her friends. At twelve, Sharon is showing irritation over such control.

> SHARON: Dad, I'm growing up, remember? How about letting me pick my own friends now.
> FATHER: You don't understand, honey. Some children are a bad influence on you.
> SHARON: You don't trust me, dad. I resent that.

FATHER: But right now we have better judgment than you.

SHARON: No way, dad. I'm not going to hang around just with kids that you want me to.

What's happening is that Sharon's parents are not losing Sharon, they are losing power over Sharon.

Children resent parental use of power. Power is the parental need to win, to be right by virtue of "who I am." If parents always win arguments with children, children grieve loss of equality with parents. Parents have authority over children, but they do not have the right to exercise power.

Compare these two parental positions.

Power

"Always remember who I am."

Sets all rules and limits, and punishes to win.

Authority

"We are equals."

Gives children a voice in setting limits.

Power punishes children and is a way for parents to get out their feelings, but the child learns nothing other than that parents have strong feelings and hit or spank very hard. With discipline, children are given reasons for having privileges withdrawn, so that something is learned about behavior that is currently unacceptable to parents.

Families, of course, must have a line of authority, for without limits on behavior, chaos would reign in the home. But as children grow, limits and rules need updating, and children should have a voice in determining the restrictions. I know some families whose teen-age children still go by the same bedtime rules they did when they were eight or ten. As children grow up, bedtime hours should move up; if not, children rebel. When a teen-ager strays from his parents' ideals, the prominent parental grief symptom is guilt: "Where have I gone wrong?" they ask. Let's look at the Jacksons, a family consisting of father, mother, and two sons, Charles and Rick. The parents came to my office to talk about Rick, the younger son, who had been an honor student and star athlete in high school. Upon graduating, Rick enrolled in college and moved out of the home. Six months into his freshman year, Rick began making "strange" phone calls home. His speech was slurred, and on several occasions Rick blurted out that he wished he were dead.

Growing suspicious that Rick was using drugs, the parents probed into his campus activities to learn that Rick was addicted to cocaine and was begging, borrowing, and stealing to support his addiction. Soon, and with no prior notice, Rick disappeared. As parents they grieved Rick's disappearance and addiction, but they grieved even more Rick's deviation from their high standards.

Children's choices may cause parents to grieve, especially those choices causing children physical and emotional damage. But parents, giving their best, can lead children only to a certain point, then the child must choose and assume responsibility for the consequences of those choices.

4. *Never force a child to talk about his grief feelings or probe with questions like "Why do you feel that way about*

the loss?" Up to the age of eleven or twelve, the child does not have the verbal sophistication to explain his feelings in order to feel understood. The best way for a grieving child to work through grief feelings is play.

For children, play is more than fun. It also offers a method for children to master overwhelming experiences. Take seven-year-old Sue, for example. Sue's parents told me that within three years the family had moved three times. With each move Sue retreated into her shell a little more. The parents related that Sue was doing poorly in school. During recess she stayed near the teacher and did not participate in games with the other children. At home Sue showed little interest in anything other than television. Sometimes she began to cry for no reason that her parents were aware of.

During the two years that I counseled Sue, she and I played with the toys, blocks, and sandbox I have in my office. I did not ask her questions to which she would have to supply answers. What mattered were her feelings. Perhaps she would express these feelings through play. When she mistrusted me, I reflected, "You don't trust me today, do you?" and when she angrily threw down a toy, I reflected that feeling too.

On one such occasion, after Sue angrily knocked over a wall of blocks she had built, we both sat in silence for a minute.

> SUE: I like to knock things down.
> I.T. That feels good to you, huh?
> SUE: I wish I was big like you so I could knock people down.

I.T. You sound angry at someone.

SUE: (Silence) When daddy doesn't listen I'd like to knock him down.

I.T. Sometimes you want daddy to understand how you feel and he's too busy or something.

The building blocks Sue knocked down represented daddy. Other days, Sue built a sand castle or arranged people in the playhouse while she talked of fear or mistrust of someone in her family. It became apparent to me that she was grieving the loss of repeated moves, losing teachers she liked and friends she made. She did not have the verbal sophistication to tell parents, "I feel very hurt or angry or mistrustful that you have moved me around so much." In fact, Sue was not even aware of grieving. With the aid of toys, we "played" her grief feelings through. Her grief softened. As it did, Sue's interest in schoolwork renewed and she began to play with other children.

A logical question to ask is if play provides the same outlet for grieving adults. Play and fun is one option anyone should employ to release grief feelings. When we grieve, we do not always feel up to having fun, but there ought to be some form of recreation to engage in. We cannot always verbalize our feelings, but we can act them out through play and fun.

5. *Do not be in a big hurry to replace children's losses.* If a loss is replaced too quickly, children conclude that love may easily be transferred and that they should put loss feelings behind them quickly. For instance, if a pet is replaced too soon, parents thwart the child's grieving process and deprive him of *his* way of mastering a painful experience.

Rushing a child through grief is like saying, "An animal can be replaced and you can love one as well as another." But if a loved one, person or pet, is easily replaced, what does a child learn about love and the permanence of things?

The time for replacing a pet, and only if the child chooses to replace it, is when grief begins to soften.

Children, I believe, moreso than adults, laud the uniqueness of each living thing. For a child there will never be another pet hamster or dog or raccoon exactly like the one that died or ran away. A different one later on maybe, but the new pet will be just that—unique.

The changes we grieve as loss, as well as our grieving patterns themselves, are established in childhood. Parents who respect children's right to grieve teach them that:

1. Loss is natural to life.
2. People and objects do not have permanence.
3. Grief feelings are normal.
4. Grief offers opportunities to help establish or reestablish values and goals.

Reflective listening, or understanding children's feelings, is necessary if they are to learn that grief feelings are normal. Parents, through listening, give children "permission" to grieve.

Part II
Mastering Our Losses

5
Everyday Losses Are Real

Dr. Erich Lindemann, professor of psychiatry at Harvard, was one of the first to show that grief comes in stages and that each stage must be worked through. In an article entitled "Symptomology and Management of Acute Grief" (1944), published in *The American Journal of Psychiatry*, he listed five stages of grief: (1) somatic distress, (2) preoccupation with the image of the deceased, (3) guilt, (4) hostile reactions, and (5) loss of patterns of conduct.

Later, Dr. Granger Westberg, enlarging on Lindemann's findings, spoke of little griefs and large griefs. "You cannot live without experiencing grief in a thousand different ways. Such a seemingly inconsequential thing as your husband's phoning at the last minute, just before guests are arriving for dinner to say he has to work late throws you into a mild form of grief. Or perhaps the boss under whom you have worked happily for ten years is suddenly transferred, and the new man is pompous and overbearing."[1]

We grieve the loss of any love, and all forms of loss have

1. Granger E. Westberg, *Good Grief* (Philadelphia: Fortress Press, 1962), p. 3.

stages of grief in common. Across the years 1973-1975, I conducted a survey on change and loss upon 200 of my students at the University of California at Davis, and American River College in Sacramento. In addition, I studied case histories of 100 clients in regards to the following "everyday" losses:

1. Personal Losses
    A role (mother, father, doctor)
    Self-image
    Habit
    Feelings
    Confidence
    Power
    Ambition
    Body figure
2. Relationship Loss
    Physical separation
        Divorce
        Death of a loved one
        Plant or tree
        Pet
        Trusted doctor, minister, etc.
    Emotional separation
        Trust in marriage, friendship
        A child or loved one to alcoholism, drug abuse
3. Geographical Loss
    Changing locations (across town, the country)
4. Career Loss
    Job firing (or promotion)
    Retirement
    Career change

5. Health Loss
    External organ
        Arm
        Leg
        Breast
        Hearing
        Eyesight
    Internal organ
        Heart surgery
        Removal of any organ
6. Environmental Loss
    Clean air
    Landscape, rivers
7. Institutional Loss
    Faith in government, democracy
    Changes in education
    Changes in religion
    Changes in family institutions and structure
8. Property Loss
    Car in accident
    Home in flood, fire, tornado
    Family heirlooms, treasures
9. Competitive Loss
    War
    Athletic contests
    Games (cards, badminton, horseshoes, etc.)
10. Seasonal loss
    Summer, fall, etc.
    Birthday
    Vacations
    Christmas

Making the Loss Real

All respondents to my study had "reacted" to one or more of these losses, though they reserved the word *grief* and a show of grief for one loss—death.

There is, I learned, no predictable response to any form of loss. In fact, one man's loss of hair caused him more grief than another's loss of a beloved relative.

Grief as a Process

Grief is a process in which we find ourselves moving from one stage to another with no clear-cut line separating the stages. There is no rhyme or reason to the stages coming and going as they do. At times one stage, thought to be finished, returns and we wonder if that is abnormal. It isn't. It's very normal.

Stages do not unfold in a predictable sequence; that is, guilt (one stage) is not riveted to space 5 or anger to space 7. Two people, then, comparing grief stages, ought not to panic if one of them has passed through a stage the other one hasn't. "I haven't gone through the anger stage yet. When does it come?" is the logical question, but grief is illogical. In some cases, we may not feel anger.

Then too, grief consists of waves, spasms, pangs. For several hours or days, we may not feel grief, then "out of the clear blue" someone we meet, something we see, a sound, a taste, ignites a spasm, and grief starts up again.

Grief softens but it never goes away completely. We do not get over a loss. A scar remains.

C. S. Lewis puts it this way: "Grief is like a bomber circling round and dropping its bombs each time the circle brings it overhead."

The main body of grief work (immediately after loss) may last for several minutes or move on in glacierlike fashion for up to two years, even beyond. Sally, divorced for three years, enrolled in a cake-decorating class but dropped out "because decorating cakes made me cry. It reminded me of baking for my husband, Todd." Marilyn tells of grieving on the day an antique dish, one handed down from her mother, cracked in the dishwasher. One year later, window-shopping, she saw a duplicate, bringing on a grief spasm.

Grief Denial

When we grieve we do not "go crazy" or have a nervous breakdown. Grief denial, not grief itself, gives us distress.

I teach semester classes on Loneliness and Its Alternative. At semester's end, tying up loose ends, many students say the greatest reward they received was a feeling of relief, hearing others express their feelings of loneliness.

Feelings about feelings induce despair. Take Sally, a divorcee, who has always thought of herself as "strong," meaning she could, in her own words, "handle any situation." Following her divorce she was surprised to learn that being alone frightened her. She dreaded coming home to an empty house, and evenings, rather than sit home alone reading or watching television, she invited herself into friends' homes or shopped. But fear was not her real problem; fear denial was. Sally was doing everything possible to escape her fear. Someone strong, she reasoned, should not be afraid. She panicked.

At this point she enrolled in my Loneliness Alternatives class and revealed her aloneness and panic to class members. Admitting her fear helped. Class members understood, assuring her that the absence of fear was not the mark of a strong person and that fear was not abnormal after a separation. Her panic slowly subsided. She is learning to accept her fear, staying home alone more often. Though still afraid, she does not "give in" by running elsewhere. Sally's example shows how fear escalates into panic over the belief that someone strong should not be afraid.

Grief is a normal and natural reacton, but feelings *about* grief can be something else. Grief cannot take its natural course when we think that our grief is abnormal, that we are odd, or that no one ever grieved as heavily before.

The Stigma of Loss

We affix a stigma to some losses, aggravating and lengthening the grief process. We pity those who have incurred the death of a loved one, but we say that divorced people have failed. The griever who carries a stigma feels the need to explain, defend, or justify himself in a pitiful waste of energy.

Stuck in Grief

We may become lodged in one stage of the grief cycle. Look at Bill, born and raised in a tiny western town. He loved that place, so much so, he did not leave often save for two successive summers when he worked as a bellhop in a hotel in Yellowstone Park. Girls frightened him, and male friendships did not come easily, though playing drums in the high school band earned him a lot of local recognition.

Upon graduating Bill was drafted into the army, only to check himself into the hospital after two months in boot camp. In treatment Bill revealed the shock he felt upon entering a bewildering new environment, of standing guard duty nights, of sleeping with fifty other men in a barracks where snoring kept him awake, of slogging through endless hours of drill—a way of life alien to him. Professional help got him through the shock of transition, however, and he "adjusted" to military life.

Like Bill, we may find that plunging into a new life-style renders us temporarily incapable of meeting the demands others put on us. We will have to first work our way through shock in the grieving process.

Major Loss—Minor Losses

Major loss, in Bill's case, was the act of leaving home. But think of his secondary losses—things such as the *privacy* of his own room, the *freedom* of coming and going as he always pleased, the *familiarity* of a comfortable routine, the *security* of his own room in which there was a hi-fi set and a set of drums. One major loss, then, spawns a network of minor losses.

Terminating a courtship gives rise to severe grief. Bille Jean, forty-five, a high school chemistry teacher, grieving loss of a two-year trial marriage, cut her wrist with a razor blade the day Don, her lover, left for good. Billie's major loss was observing Don pack his belongings and drive away. Begging him to stay, she was in shock for a day before crying. After the actual loss, she went into the house where, alone, she began to think of her secondary losses: a companion, a stimulating conversationalist, a loss of *dreams*. "What I will miss most," she confided "is being held close by someone I love."

Billie will need to explore new ways of structuring her time to include being with people in order to prevent boredom and fulfill her need to love and be loved.

We cannot predict, prior to a major loss, what our secondary losses will be. Separation brings secondary losses to light. Following her divorce, one woman told me she missed tending a small orchard in her backyard, one she planted and nursed along for years. Another divorcee said she grieved loss of the family cat, kept by her husband. Bitter feelings arose between them over "cat visitation rights." The final agreement was that he would keep the cat, though she could have the cat on weekends. We may feel embarrassed grieving what others feel are little losses. They are big to us.

Loss and Physical Disease

In the 1930s Harold G. Wolff, a neurologist at the Cornell University Medical College and New York University, began studying the onset of illness. Five thousand persons were asked to tell about life events that preceded their illnesses. They reported a wide range of events—death of a spouse, a visit by a mother-in-law, a change of job, the birth of a child.[2] It was discovered that life events help cause many diseases, including colds, tuberculosis, and skin disease.

Later Wolff and his colleague, Dr. Thomas Holmes, of the University of Washington School of Medicine, did a study of patients who had colds and nasal infections, asking them, when they came in for medical care, to come back when they had recovered. When each patient returned, blood flow, freedom of breathing, swelling, and secretion in the nose were measured. Then the patient was asked about the event or events that had occurred before he became ill. After a conversation about a mother-in-law, for instance, or retirement, the measurements were repeated. Discussion of the event renewed the old symptoms. In fact, so many patients mentioned mother-in-law visits that Wolff and Holmes began to consider them a common cause of disease in the United States.

Excited by their findings, they studied thousands of tuberculosis patients and found out that tuberculosis tends to strike persons who are caught up in dramatic life changes and who feel hopelessly overwhelmed. Most were ordinary events of everyday life—change in school, change in financial state, personal illness. But the single factor common to all tuberculosis patients was change—desirable or undesirable—in ongoing life patterns.

Later, in a study with Richard H. Rahe and other colleagues at the University of Washington School of

2. Thomas Holmes and Minoru Masuda, "Psychosomatic Syndrome," *Psychology Today*, April 1972, p. 71.

Medicine, it was revealed that life events clustered in a two-year period before the onset of tuberculosis, heart disease, skin disease, and hernia. And women—married or un-married—tend to become pregnant at times of great life change.

Next they set up a scale to guide them in predicting the onset of disease. In all, 394 persons were asked to rate the amount of social readjustment required for each of the forty-three changes in life patterns. A numerical value of 500 was assigned to one event, marriage. Subjects were given the following instructions:

> As you complete each of the remaining events, think to yourself: "Is this event indicative of more or less readjustment than marriage?" "Would the readjustment take longer or shorter to accomplish?" If you decide the readjustment is more intense and protract-ed, choose a proportionately larger number for the event. If you decide the readjustment required is less than marriage then choose a proportionately smaller number for the event.[3]

The results showed agreement about the rating of the life events. The event requiring the greatest amount of social readjustment was death of spouse, which was then assigned a mean value of 100. All other life events were then assigned mean values relative to the loss of a spouse. The results were as follows:

3. Ibid., p. 72.

Rank	Life Event	Mean Value
1	Death of spouse	100
2	Divorce	73
3	Marital separation	65
4	Jail term	63
5	Death of close family member	63
6	Personal injury or illness	53
7	Marriage	50
8	Fired at work	47
9	Marital reconciliation	45
10	Retirement	45
11	Change in health of family member	44
12	Pregnancy	40
13	Sex difficulties	39
14	Gain of new family member	39
15	Business readjustment	39
16	Change in financial state	38
17	Death of close friend	37
18	Change to different line of work	36
19	Change in number of arguments with spouse	35
20	Mortgage over $10,000	31
21	Foreclosure of mortgage or loan	30
22	Change in responsibilities at work	29
23	Son or daughter leaving home	29
24	Trouble with in-laws	29
25	Outstanding personal achievement	28
26	Wife begins or stops work	26
27	Beginning or end of school	26
28	Change in living conditions	25
29	Revision of personal habits	24
30	Trouble with boss	23

Rank	Life Event	Mean Value
31	Change in work hours or conditions	20
32	Change in residence	20
33	Change in schools	20
34	Change in recreation	19
35	Change in church activities	19
36	Change in social activities	18
37	Mortgage or loan less than $10,000	17
38	Change in sleeping habits	16
39	Change in number of family get-togethers	15
40	Change in eating habits	15
41	Vacation	13
42	Christmas	13
43	Minor violations of the law	11

No particular event seemed linked to a particular disease. The important point was the total impact of life events and the coping behavior that was required. The more serious crises brought on the most serious diseases.

If, then, we are aware that stress and feelings of loss bring on disease and that personal attitudes shape our reaction to change, we can choose to assume greater responsibility for our attitudes toward change. For example, if we are aware that we are fighting the aging process tooth and nail, we should also see that any change in our physical appearance is grieved as loss. If we grow weary of such grievings, we can work to modify our attitude toward aging. One way is to closely examine our body image—the mental image we have of our bodies. We must ask ourselves, "Do I value myself for appearance only? Do I feel loved for looks and dress alone?" If feelings of self-worth are based on appearance only, we may need professional help to modify that attitude.

Similarly, when we realize that we are holding prejudice that the "good old days" were best and resisting all change within the current social structure, we can choose to evaluate new life-styles and philosophies. No one is a victim of change. If we are unhappy with our attitude toward change, we can choose to change our attitude.

Fred enrolled in college intent upon becoming a chemist, but in his freshman year, he failed two science courses and gave up the engineering program. Grieving this change and loss, he blamed the teacher for being too strict; in fact he went a step further and said he would have made the grade in a different school. He then decided to become a minister but eventually dropped out of that because "people in the program were too square for me." In both instances, Fred blamed others for his changes and losses. We are responsible for the consequences of our choices. If we blame others for our losses, we remain irresponsible for our decisions.

6
The Stages of Grief

There are feelings and stages common to all forms of loss—up to eleven in all: shock, sobbing, craziness, relief, physical symptoms of unresolved grief, panic, guilt, anger, limbo, hope emerges, reality is reaffirmed. One respondent, a female, passed through all upon removal of a cancerous breast. Another, a nineteen-year-old male freshman suffering from homesickness, reported working through shock, sobbing, panic, anger, and guilt.

The Stage of Shock

Following a loss, our initial reaction is mild or severe shock: We feel *speechless* upon failing the chemistry exam. We *cannot believe* a close friend was arrested for arson. We are *dumbfounded* over our dentist moving.

Shock serves as a cushion, giving us time to absorb the *fact of loss*. We hear the words of loss, but we do not *feel* the loss.

At midnight once I received a telephone call from the

county coroner requesting I inform a woman that her husband had just been killed in a freeway collision. I went. That was hard news to break to her in the dead of night. Upon hearing of the loss, she gasped and sank into a chair where she sat speechless for an hour. Then she sobbed.

Another day, this time in the hospital, I heard a doctor inform a woman her baby had been born with a webbed foot, and she was begging him to say he had told the wrong mother.

Shock wanes only as rapidly as our capacity to absorb loss feelings. That rate differs in each of us.

The Stage of Sobbing

As shock softens, permitting loss feelings to sink in, we sob. Sobbing often assumes the form of wailing, the uttermost symbol of human agony.

Crying is different, centered more in our throat. When I sense that a grieving patient needs to sob, I often pull over a large pillow I keep in my office and request that the patient lie across it, face down. This position removes restrictions within the chest and throat areas, enabling sobbing energy to emerge freely. Sobbing is as violent a release of energy as is vomiting a release of physical energy.

The prospect of sobbing frightens us because we "will not be able to stop." We fear losing control of ourselves, even disintegrating. Bob grieves the loss of trust in his wife, June, after her affair with a neighbor. He talks of the loss with a pinched voice, evidence of controlling his feelings. "If I ever began sobbing, I won't be able to quit," he repeats. To sob,

Bob will probably need the *protection* of someone holding him, someone he trusts, assuring him his feelings are acceptable. Meanwhile Bob channels his energy into denial of sobbing.

The Stage of Physical Symptoms

Physical symptoms of unresolved grief may emerge anytime during the grief cycle. Temporary paralysis of a limb, vomiting, insomnia, diarrhea, trembling, even temporary blindness—all are symptoms of unresolved grief. Chest pains are also common.

Upon the onset of these symptoms, we may panic. In order to make certain our symptoms do or do not stem from unresolved grief, we should always check with our doctor. Medication may be required.

Marilyn is grieving the marriage of her daughter, Julie, an only child. Throughout high school, the mother and daughter frequently golfed together and held long discussions on a variety of subjects. Marilyn depended upon Julie to fulfill her emotional and intellectual needs. Julie's marriage, then, was a severe loss to her mother. A physical symptom of Marilyn's grief emerged one day as she was driving on the freeway. "Suddenly I didn't know where I was so I panicked and pulled over to the side of the road. Ever since I've been afraid to drive." A thorough physical checkup failed to reveal any physical base for her disorientation. The attack was a manifestation of grief.

At one time people believed that grief was a cause of death. Back in 1657, Dr. Heberden, an English physician, classified the causes of death in London like this:

Flox and Small Pox 835
French Pox 25
Gout 8
Grief 10
Gripe and Plague in the Guts 446

The term *brokenhearted* has its origin in the book of Isaiah, "Bind up the brokenhearted," and ever since the idea has persisted that severe grief can somehow damage the heart and even bring on death. Benjamin Rush, the American physician, writing in *Medical Inquiries and Observations upon the Diseases of the Mind* (1836) said: "Dissection of persons who have died shows congestion in and inflammation of the heart with rupture of its auricles and ventricles."[1]

In the wake of loss, grief weakens our resistance to illness, which may lead to death, but no one has yet proven that grief of itself is the direct cause of death.

The Stage of Rationalizing

Rationalizing "it could have been worse" helps us bear grief, but overrationalizing hinders the grieving process.

It is normal to compare our loss to someone else's and to conclude they are much worse off then we. We then tend to dismiss our loss as small by comparison and feel ashamed for grieving: "I only lost my job, he lost his wife."

Comparing losses is normal. If we search long enough, we can always find someone whose loss seems more

1. Colin Murray Parkes, *Bereavement, Studies in Grief in Adult Life* (New York: International Studies Press, 1973).

traumatic than ours. But even when that is our conclusion, we should not feel guilty for grieving, or worse, deny our grief.

The Stage of Craziness

During the early stages of grief, our judgment is faulty. We jump to conclusions. We make hasty decisions over which we are often sorry later.

Deciding to change locations while in shock is unwise. A cardinal rule of grief is: Never make decisions about *moving* or *money* while in shock. A couple I know has moved from rural Kansas to Los Angeles and back to Kansas again two times in three years. They do not give themselves time to work through the shock of changing locations. Instead, they make a decision to move when *in* shock. Changing locations has both losses and gains. At first we are frequently more aware of the losses and things we "miss." But as time passes and the shock of loss wears off, we become aware of gains.

Lynn Caine writes of her craziness following the death of her husband, Martin, of setting the table for two, of going to the supermarket—"Oh, they have endive today, I'd better get some for Martin"—of running after someone in the street that looked like Martin, of reaching for the phone to dial Martin at work, of renewing a subscription to Martin's car magazine. "I had a sense of Martin, of some quality of Martin that had filtered into me. A very real feeling part of me was Martin."[2]

2. Lynn Caine, *Widow* (New York: William Morrow and Co., 1974), p 102.

Part of grief is believing reality can be repeated, that our wishing will bring back the person or that we will find a facsimile of the lost one.

A disappointing thing about returning home from college for the first time is that we expect to find people and places unchanged; that teachers, friends, old hangouts, even parents, will be the same. But everything changes. Many college freshmen grieve these "losses."

The Stage of Relief

Our losses are accompanied by a degree of relief. But often we say nothing of our relief, fearing that others will say we are calloused or "crazy." A doctor told me that six months after his son Jack was killed he felt relief and wondered if he was "cracking up." He went on to explain that Jack had been a problem teen-ager, had run away from home repeatedly, had been arrested twice, and was killed while driving the family car in an intoxicated state. "I feel relieved of worrying over his safety and wondering what was going to happen to him next," the father explained.

This father's relief does not imply he didn't love his son. He loved him dearly and was plagued by guilt after his death, wondering what he could have done to help Jack avert so much turmoil. But as his initial grief reaction softened, he could not deny feeling relieved for he would be *spared* anxiety.

My father hovered between life and death for two weeks after a massive heart attack. He fought valiently to live for he was not old by today's standards—only sixty-three—and he longed to fulfill dreams of travel and retirement. But he died. Had he lived, the doctor told us, he would have been confined to home the rest of his life, a near invalid. I, of course qrieved. But time enabled me to see that had he lived he would have chafed under the doctor's restrictions. In the sense of the suffering he was spared, I felt relief.

It is this *sparing* aspect of loss over which we feel relief. We may become aware of relief after a child leaves for college. As much as we love our children and miss them, we are *spared* things upon their departure. Take, for instance, the matter of monitoring the length of teen telephone calls. Despite a firm rule that Vicki and Bob are allotted ten minutes per phone call, they invariably forget, making it necessary for parents to remind and remind and remind. Raising children consists not so much of teaching them new things as reminding them of what they have already been told. "If I've told you once, I've told you a thousand times" is a familiar statement of exasperation in every family. Or take the matter of parents lying awake at night waiting for their teen-ager to return from a date or with the family car. As much as we want them to have fun and *do* trust them, we still find ourselves checking the clock and imagining the worst as the curfew hour approaches. When the child leaves home, we will, of course, miss him. Nonetheless, we feel *some* relief. We won't have to wait up worrying about them anymore.

Nearly always, following a divorce, either one partner or the other feels a degree of relief. If *he* has periodically beaten *her*, then *she* feels relief from the fear of abuse and the actual pummeling. Or if arguments have been fierce and financial commitments overwhelming, the absence of these battles is a relief.

Our relief may be humorous to one hearing us relate it. Said one divorcee, "At least there is one consolation. I'll be spared scooping up after the dog in the backyard now." Serious or funny (to others) our relief is genuine. More than once we feel relief from the petty irritations and small annoyances about the other.

As much as we grieve loss of a job, relief feelings that crop up often surprise us. Stu, employed as a milk truck driver for twelve years, was dismissed. For twelve years, Stu had retired at 7:30 P.M. each evening and arisen at 2:30 A.M., missing many family activities. Now he would feel more a part of family life. In addition, the foreman and he had frequent spats. He would be spared that irritation.

Must we always feel relief? Of course not. Loss circumstances differ. But if we do, we should not feel guilty or question our sanity.

The Panicky Stage

We may come to the point in grief where the agony seems intolerable. We want to run—anywhere. We can think of nothing but the loss. We even dream of it, for dreams are an avenue for grief expression. At work our employer is irritated over our absentmindedness, and family members' patience is wearing thin with our listlessness. The situation seems hopeless. Our thinking is muddled and fears of entering a mental hospital plague us.

Panic is normal, though we can be spared much of it if we know that no one ever "went crazy" grieving.

Going crazy is an unfortunate term. It connotes a mental

picture of being strapped to a bed in a mental hospital or, if free to move, pounding on walls or running wildly down the street screaming and ranting. Internal upheaval during grief is normal. Our minds are jumbled, and we feel at the mercy of our feelings. In short, self-control seems to be slipping away and that feeling frightens us. The alternative to losing control is fantasizing ourselves as wild lunatics requiring physical restraints. Clinging to that fantasy, our panic mounts. If our panic seems intolerable, we will need to do something to release our panic energy. Talking about our feelings may help or getting busy with something or sobbing. Screaming, some people tell me, affords relief— driving to a remote spot and then simply "letting go." Screaming, of course, is an act we equate with "going crazy," so few of us employ that form of release. But more of us should. The presence of a trusted friend gives us *permission* and *protection* enabling us to "let go." Permission is giving encouragement in a statement like, "It's okay to get your feelings out through screaming." Protection is given during the act of screaming (or sobbing, whatever the feeling may be) by (1) touching or holding, (2) verbal reassurance, (3) mere presence. If our friend accepts and values our mode of expression, we can trust it too.

Emotional and physical fatigue during grief contributes to panic. We need to resist the temptation to skip meals or, when we do eat, to consume food laced with sugar and carbohydrates. Proper nutrition, even though we eat sparingly, is vital during grief.

Lack of sleep alone saps a major portion of our energy required to grieve. If our sleeping pattern deteriorates rapidly during grief, we may need to consult our doctor for a sedative to restore our pattern. I do not believe in prescribing a sedative during the grieving process unless it is cause for considering a prescribed sedative.

The temptation during grief is to sit, if not to just sit and stare, then to watch television or maybe read. Regular exercise, therefore, is mandatory, for it induces relaxation and generates hunger. I cannot stress enough the need to maintain sufficient sleep and sound eating habits during grief. If our physical energy flags, so does our emotional endurance.

If there is ever a time in life when we feel like "doing nothing," it is during grief. We will have to force ourselves some days to exercise or go to a movie or go to work. Yes, we will have to "act as if." In doing so, I am not suggesting we deny our grief but that we give our grief balance by doing all we can to maintain our regular activities and schedule. "Acting as if" is not pretending we are not grieving but thwarting our urge to just sit and do nothing.

The Stage of Guilt

Guilt has two parts: true and false. I am not saying that true guilt is authentic and false guilt artificial. Both feelings are authentic. Let me explain.

True guilt is remorse over a lost opportunity. Here is an eighth grade student, Tracy, who neglects to prepare for a final history exam. She feels confident of passing, so confident, in fact, she attends a party the evening before, going to bed at 2:00 A.M. She flunks the exam and grieving says, "If I had taken advantage of the opportunity to prepare, I would have passed with flying colors. But now it's too late." Tracy, feeling guilty, grieves loss of an opportunity.

We grieve lost opportunities within relationships. One of

the most frequent instances of true guilt occurs within offspring after a parent dies. Now it is too late to express appreciations felt but withheld. Of a mate who dies, the survivor often laments, "We should have gone to Europe as we planned." It isn't until the moment of separation that we become aware of all the lost opportunities.

False guilt is shouldering responsibility for the loss and blaming ourselves all out of proportion. Take, for instance, the case of John, a heart attack victim at age thirty-four. An ambitious executive, he worked thirteen hours daily, smoking two packs of cigarettes daily, and was careless about the treatment of high blood pressure. His wife, Claudine, said regretfully, "Had I warned him more often he might have slowed down." But it was John who chose to burn the candle at both ends. Whenever the breadwinner falls victim to illness, family members struggle through a period of self-blame and guilt.

We should not, as in the case of John's wife, attempt to "talk her out" of guilt. Time will soften it. Everyone other than John's wife may see she is not to blame for his illness and show disgust over her insistence on self-blame. But when we lose someone we love, we ponder every conceivable course of action we could have taken (or not taken) to prevent the loss.

Jo, a friend, will understand Claudia's guilt:

> CLAUDIA: Jo, it's terrible to feel so guilty about something. How can I ever forgive myself for not insisting John take better care of himself?
> JO: It's hard not to blame yourself and reflect back to what you could and should have done.

CLAUDIA: That's right. I saw him getting more wound up this past year, but I didn't say a word.
JO: So you're feeling "if I had only."

Jo is not trying to talk Claudia out of her feelings, knowing that time will soften them and the understanding of friends like herself will help.

Contrast Jo's response to that of Barbara, another of Claudia's friends.

CLAUDIA: Barbara, I know that had I insisted on John slowing down he would have.
BARBARA: How do you know that. It may have gotten you two fighting.
CLAUDIA: I doubt it. He usually listens to me, but I thought he was big enough to take care of himself.
BARBARA: Right on, I'll buy that. He chose to drive himself to a heart atack, and I think you're smart enough to understand that, Claudia.
CLAUDIA: I guess I'm not. I've rationalized this whole thing half to death, but I still feel guilty.
BARBARA: I hestitate saying this, dear, but God helps them who help themselves.

The irony of Barbara's response, that Mike chose to work too hard, is true: Mike did choose. Yet, Barbara is using that truth to "talk Claudia out" of her feelings, thus frustrating Claudia even more. Claudia knows one thing (Mike did choose), but she feels something else, and that is her conflict. Barbara can best help Claudia's feeling to soften by understanding it, not trying to "talk her out" of her guilt, thus making her feel guilty over feeling guilty.

The Stage of Anger

This state, if it does emerge, usually comes near the middle or toward the end of the grief cycle. Immediately after loss, we are preoccupied with ourselves (what we could have done to prevent the loss or our feelings of helplessness). But as grief softens and confidence rises, our minds switch to others and what they should or could have done to prevent the loss from occurring.

Blame may range anywhere from the example of a mother who upon learning her daughter did not pass first grade points the finger of blame at the entire educational system, to parents who upon hospitalization of an emotionally disturbed daughter charge, "If the psychiatrist had prescribed the right medication in time hospitalization could have been avoided."

In both cases, the charge may in part be true. But establishing blame does not bring back the lost person, pet, or object. Blaming another is sometimes a way of feeling less guilty ourselves. But most often it is simply a normal reaction to the loss of anything we love.

Mark and Ede were married during his freshman year in medical school. Ede supported them both by working as a stenographer. After graduation, Mark set up practice in a small rural town. Ede volunteered to be his secretary. "We worked together," she recalls. "I billed patients, made appointments, even scrubbed the wash basins." Five years passed, then he requested a divorce. "I was furious," says Ede, "furious because he left me to raise our two daughters. And what's more, I wanted to reap some of the creature comforts of my long investment in the business, too." She speaks angrily of him as a "checkbook father," sending money to support them but assuming no other responsibilities. Her bank will not issue her a loan "because a single female parent cannot get credit." Her unresolved anger shows in physical symptoms—gagging during meals and migraine headaches.

We should not be flabbergasted if grieving friends "dump" unresolved anger on us, even if we are blameless for their loss. Grief is irrational and impulsive outbursts of blame are often aimed at the nearest person. As a counselor I am the recipient of much unresolved anger.

Should a couple choose not to work out their differences, rather than blame each other, they may blame me, saying I am incompetent, don't care, or that I took sides with the other.

After a loss, if we do not give ourselves adequate grieving time, the result is we vent unresolved grief—anger mainly— on a new friend or mate. A couple married but two months came to see me once, and after one hour, I saw the reason the marriage stood on the verge of toppling. Unresolved anger from the wife's first marriage was spilling over into her new marriage. Her new husband was the recipient of anger that she should have directed at her first husband.

Unresolved grief often serves as the initial attraction between two freshly divorced persons. Finally "someone understands how I feel and what I have gone through." Each pours out upon the other unexpressed grief feelings.

Concluding they have a lot in common, they marry. But unresolved grief, though mutual, is shaky common ground upon which to base a marriage. Reason: They may know little about each other, other than grief feelings. And sometimes concentrating on the past is an avoidance technique for risking present reactions to each other. Marriages based only upon a foundation of unresolved grief seldom work.

When Grief Softens

The day arrives when grief softens. The space between our grief pangs is lengthening. Whereas before our pangs were nearly constant, now they are stretched further apart. A spasm today is less intense than a spasm last week. Hope returns. We are going to "make it" after all; we will survive.

7
Is Grief Depression?

Most doctors lump grief—major or minor—into one classification: *reactive depression*. The term means exactly what it says: depression in reaction to some life event. This singular diagnosis, however, fails to recognize that grief is a normal reaction to loss and so every grieving ought not to be automatically classified as depression.

There are multiple types of depression, beginning with the normal "blaahs" or "blues," a feature of Monday morning. We dread going to work but once we've gotten through Monday morning our spirits perk up. Our depression is situational; we know its cause and when it will end.

An endogenous depression is inner confusion over loss of personal identity, the "who am I?" struggle. Losing an election to a seat on the city council can cause unresolved personality conflict to surface. Counseling treatment may be required in which the counselee grows to understand his ambivalent feelings, leading to a clearer personal identity.

Another form of depression is called simply a depressive illness. Treatment is antidepressant medication and short-term therapy. It frequently strikes persons with no history of depression. As mysteriously as it came, it leaves, and it may never return again.

The last type of depression is psychotic depression. It may be accompanied by hallucinations. There is a direct, identifiable object loss and treatment is through counseling and medication. A comparison of grief to depression is made by David Peretz:

> The grief stricken person will, within a short period of time after the loss, show shifts of moods within the same day. In contrast the depressed person will be more persistently downcast, although his depression may subside toward evening each day. The grieving person may respond to warmth and reassurance, the mildly depressed person may respond to pressure, promises and urging. The more severely depressed will be relatively unresponsive to most stimuli and will sit huddled and downcast in gloom.[1]

Grief can grow morbid, the point where professional help is needed to become unstuck. These points are listed in a later chapter.

Can We Prepare for Loss?

We prepare intellectually for loss, not to thwart our grief when loss comes but to gather facts to help us grieve

1. Bernard Schoenberg et al, eds., *Loss and Grief, Psychological Management in Medical Practice* (New York and London: Columbia University Press, 1970), p. 29.

without shame or apology. For example, preparation for retirement should begin in middle life when we decide on retirement location, income required to subsist, trips to take, even reading a book or two on feelings to expect. But when retirement day arrives and the fact of loss hits us we will grieve because *grief is a feeling reaction to loss*.

Is there one successful method of working through grief that "works" for everybody? Unfortunately, there is not. The grieving process is always in flux. What helps most to soften grief changes daily. We will have to "play it by ear."

Grief has its own unique rhythm, an ebb and flow that cannot be *directed* or contained by our willpower. We cannot get over grief by gritting our teeth and declaring, "I will not feel angry over the loss today." Laboring to conjure up a desired feeling is futile, and upon discovering we cannot, our despair compounds. Grief feelings do not respond to internal commands.

One mode of grief expression is talking our feelings out. Feelings are energy. We cannot think our feelings "away"; feelings dissipate through verbal or physical activity. Grieving people often say they need to get away to "think things through." Grief, though, is a feeling reaction to loss and while getting away affords us a welcome change of pace for several days, remember: Grief cannot be intellectualized away or thought through.

Paul Tournier said that no one can develop without feeling understood by at least one other person. Talking about our grief feelings, we do not ask the listener for advice, a pep talk, agreement, or disagreement, but understanding. Intellectual probing, "Why do you feel that way?" forces the griever to think, thus curbing his feelings. In addition, it puts the griever on the defensive, for he feels compelled to explain his feelings, defend them, even apologize for them.

If the listener feels uncomfortable with feelings, he may seek to control the griever's feelings with *why* questions.

If the listener does respond, he reflects the griever's feelings in short reactions like "You're really struggling with guilt today, aren't you?" Other times "oh" or "I see" is sufficient. The listener's task is to encourage the griever to feel the full force of his feelings. Once he does he relaxes. It frequently happens that we do not cry or display anger until we first talk of our feelings. *Talking puts us in touch with our feelings.*

If our grieving is intense, talking about our feelings may not provide sufficient release. I think of Ed, bankrupt after losing a furniture business and entrenched in the anger stage of grief. A baseball fan, he releases anger at baseball games through booing and shouting at umpires and players. Athletic contests like hockey, rugby, basketball, football, and soccer offer the participant and spectator an excellent forum for releasing grief energy, anger mainly. The *feel* and *sound* of contact dissipates grief anger; I stress sound, the *clattering* of bowling pins, the *crack* of a golf shot, the *crunch* of football contact. A man grieving divorce told me of losing his wife to a suitor. "I was so enraged I wanted to kill him," he said. Recognizing his need to explode into rage, he enrolled in an evening karate course and unleashed his wrath through shouting, grunting, and chopping.

In handball and tennis, we *hit* something, feel and hear contact. The same holds true of table tennis and croquet. The release we choose hinges on the force of our feelings and our state of health. Someone with a heart problem will not choose to play handball.

Playing a musical instrument may help. A twenty-one-year-old fellow, Jay, grieving a navy medical discharge, has taken up his drums again to help dissipate anger over the discharge. His story: After two months in boot camp, medics determined Jay had arthritic knees, saying he faced the possibility of discharge. On boot camp graduation day the company commander confirmed Jay's worst fears: He *was* being discharged. "It isn't fair," says Jay, "they could have assigned me a light job. I wanted to make the navy my career." Since his discharge, Jay has served prison time for two thefts, angry acts rooted in unexpressed grief anger over the untimely discharge. Currently on parole, Jay is choosing constructive ways to release his anger. "Talking helps," he notes "but what *really* helps is playing drums in a rock-and-roll band."

A third way grief heals is through time. Doctors remind us that medicine does not heal, medicine restores the body's capacity to heal itself. Time is the great healer. Therefore, on days we feel sure our grief will never soften, we can take heart; time is working to heal.

8
When Alone Becomes Lonely

After the loss of any love, not only persons but objects and property, we feel alone. In addition we are made aware of our ultimate aloneness.

A large share of grief is self-pity. We are forced to assess our new state of being and the changes to be made within ourselves if we are to adjust to the loss. At first that awareness may frighten, even panic, us. How are we ever going to do it? The task seems overwhelming. We feel helpless. The secret to "adjusting" will lie in deciding on a list of priorities—what needs to be done first, then second, and so on. It is when we do not set priorities that we panic.

We sometimes confuse aloneness with loneliness. Alone is not necessarily lonely. Aloneness is our state of being after a *physical* separation from a loved person, place, pet, or object. We *are* alone. Some of us are basic loners; we choose aloneness as a life-style. We choose to remain single. We are not bored, and our needs to love and be loved are fulfilled and that is a responsible form of aloneness.

An aloneness life-style is often suspect. We wonder

"what is wrong" with such people. Do they have something against marriage? Are they homosexual? We ought to refrain from judging those who choose aloneness as a lifestyle.

A basic loner has grown to like himself—what he thinks and feels. Disliking what we think and feel, we shun aloneness, for alone we are fully aware of our inner misery.

Some basic loners choose to marry but continue their retreats into aloneness, causing the mate to wonder, "What is wrong with me?" A marriage may end over this. Had husband and wife understood that individual needs for aloneness differ and that one was not rejecting the other, the marriage could have been saved. A relationship in which two are forged together 90 percent of the time is unhealthy. We smother each other, mistaking togetherness for intimacy. Within any relationship there must be a balance between aloneness and intimacy, between togetherness and closeness. Each needs time to pursue interests and hobbies. Friendship is not ownership. A friend gives us the freedom to develop in ways of our own choosing.

Some of us who live alone have loved deeply in the past. Because all love eventually ends in the suffering of separation and grief, we cannot risk another commitment. Separation through death is not always our most grievous loss. Death is final separation. We will not see the lost one again. A "living death" is separation after which two have intermittent contact. They may continue to shop in the same store, attend the same church, bowl in the same league. With divorce, the settling of legal matters requires occasional conferences between the estranged couple, and the matter of children's weekend visitation privileges finds mother and father crossing paths. Each contact is a reminder of the past, of good times and bad, keeping grief alive.

Having loved and "lost," and then having decided that loving is not worth the grief of future separations, we isolate ourselves. "What if we risk love and the friend moves away or dies?" Or, "What if we are rejected?" If we choose to risk neither giving nor receiving love, we cannot feel sorry for ourselves. *Our aloneness has spiraled into loneliness and it is of our own doing.*

It is helpful to remember that nobody can reject us, we choose to feel rejected. Should a friend decide to sever our relationship and choose a different direction, he does it as a step *toward* something or someone else and not as a step *away* from ourselves. Rejection is an attitude we take toward ourselves: "I'm not lovable." Sometimes personalities clash, even within a long-term relationship in which both have gradually grown in different directions. This doesn't mean one is right, the other wrong, or that one is superior to the other. It does mean, however, that mutual needs are no longer complimentary.

When George and Renee married, George was very dependent upon her. In the first years of marriage, Renee budgeted the family finances and even made repairs around the house that George said he could not make. Outside of his work, George had no interest in fun or people. But as time passed he slowly developed interests in hunting and golf. He also joined a hiking club that took Saturday excursions. Renee's interests stayed pretty much the same. One day George realized he was changing and so was his attitude toward Renee, for he now saw her in a different light. Before, he admired her sense of responsibility and relished her waiting on him hand and foot; now he came to resent these qualities about her, saying she was rigid, a workaholic, and had no fun. George filed for divorce. "He rejected me," Renee grieved. Actually, he hadn't. What George once *needed*—a wife to coddle him—he no longer needed. He had chosen a different direction and the person Renee was and is no longer meets his needs. We all change and as we do, so does the nature of our relationships. This does not mean that we always end the friendship. The secret of a healthy relationship is giving the other freedom to grow in his/her own way.

Separation from objects initiates feelings of aloneness. Objects become our companions by virtue of the time and energy we invest in them. A woman living alone sold her handsome thirty-year-old piano to pay off delinquent bills. The piano stood in her parlor all those years. She gave lessons on it to hundreds of students, derived pleasure from practicing on it. After the piano was wheeled away, she felt an emptiness in her house and within herself.

Loss brings to life feelings of deprivation. The departure of a person, pet, or object means that the object fulfilling our needs is gone.

Of deprivation, C. S. Lewis writes: "I am beginning to understand why grief feels like suspense. It comes from the frustration of so many impulses that had been habitual. Thought after thought, feeling after feeling, action after action had Helen for their target. Now their target is gone. I keep on, through habit, fitting an arrow to the string, then I remember and I have to lay the bow down."[1]

1. C. S. Lewis, *A Grief Observed* (Greenwich, Conn.: Seabury Press, 1961), p. 7.

Anything responding to our giving validates our worth. I don't know of a better definition of life than the one summing it up as stimuli and response. Beginning at conception, we are "acted upon," stirred to life by forces outside ourselves—by love, food, and water. That we have this marvelous capacity to respond is proof we are alive, as when infants chuckle when tickled, coo when rocked, tremble at loud voices.

When our capacity to respond flickers, life itself flickers, as it did with Snowball, a white rabbit I brought home from a farm one day to our three daughters who were all under five years then. For a year the girls heaped love on Snowball, amazed he'd respond. Each time a girl, lugging water in one hand, clutching a carrot in the other, approached the wire mesh pen, Snowball's nose wiggled and his tail fluttered. But Snowball got sick one day. In spite of our best efforts to pull him through, his response capacity waned. Nothing seemed to help, not even the antibiotic a veterinarian injected into his trembling little body. Snowball died. My wife and I grieved right along with the kids.

We cherish pets because their response to our stroking is so predictable. Stroke a stray cat and what happens?—he follows us anywhere. Or a dog, he leaps all over us, licking our face.

One man whose dog was crushed by a car said, "That dog was my whole life." Several of his neighbors chided him for that remark, charging he loved animals more than people. But everywhere that man walked, to the post office, or hunting, his faithful dog had padded along behind.

Our need for validation begins at birth. Wise parents praise the creative works of their children, the poems and hand-drawn pictures brought home from school, taping them to the refrigerator, or pinning them to the bulletin board. Parents' responses to childrens gifts assures children their giving has worth.

During their preschool years a child's primary need is to be loved. But at the age of five or six, if parents validate children's *giving experiments*, new awareness peeps through in their minds: Something *feels better* than being loved—loving. And while loving is risky (the response cannot be predicted), when there is a positive response that feeling is unparalleled in life. The part of ourselves we gave—a compliment, touch, or smile—brought forth a response from within another.

Plants' responses help validate our worth. I know a woman, living alone at eighty, whose hobby is nursing dying plants back to life. They stand in rows of four and five on windowsills where the sun touches the leaves. She knows when and how to fertilize each plant and when to water them. Whenever a plant exhibits a spark of life one would think the greatest thing in the world had happened. To her it has; that response validates the worth of her giving.

Roses we have nurtured, humming birds drinking from feeders we've filled, squirrels plucking peanuts from between our fingers—all of these responses validate the worth of our giving. Small wonder we react to the loss of anything we have given to and received from.

The greatest frustration of single parents who are raising children is the absence of another adult to validate the fairness of rules and limits, and in addition, their reaction to the children's behavior. When the single parent thinks, "I'm so angry I could strangle the kids," he wonders, "Am I sick?" The bulk of my counseling work with single parents consists of validating the "normalcy" of their reactions to children.

Your Capacity to Love

If aloneness is our reaction to loss then loneliness is our reaction to feeling deprived of those "essential materials" the loved one provided us with.

Karl Menninger, with characteristic insight, said that the curing of mental and emotional illness is restoring one's *capacity* to love. If we decide that love is not worth the risk of eventual separation our capacity to love dies. Losing that capacity is our most excruciating form of grief.

Some of us dread even a temporary good-bye. Pat relates her dread of flying to Hawaii to visit a daughter "because I cannot stand saying good-bye at the end of the visit. Am I odd?" she asks me. Pat is not odd. She was raised in a military family where the nature of her father's assignments required the family to move fifteen times in twenty years. Each time Pat grieved loss of friends, teachers, houses, and the security of belonging.

There are seven levels of deprivation and loneliness:

1. *Presence deprivation.* Constructive verbal communication, when and how to fight, is the theme of many books nowadays. But what of our need to simply "be with" someone we trust when touching or talking violates the intimacy we seek?

At the age of eleven I went through a period where after

going to bed at night I called out to my parents, "Are you still out there?" I didn't desire conversation; I just wanted to be reassured of their presence.

Entering the house after school, glancing about and inquiring, "Is anybody home?" children need to know someone is there—if not mother or father then a brother or sister. If that is impossible, a pet helps. Otherwise children feel deprived of presence. Coming home to an empty house, regardless of age, is lonely.

Individual needs for presence differ. Some say it is during the evening hours between 5:00 P.M. and 7:00 P.M., at bedtime, on holidays, Saturday, Sunday, a birthday, or a rainy day. If we understand our needs for presence, we can plan ahead.

Presence alternatives are not absolutes, however, but shades of gray. Diane, a divorcee, needs presence at bedtime, so she sleeps on the couch with her back against the soft cushions. Other people have a dog or cat or a large pillow with them on the bed.

2. *Intellectual deprivation.* We need another with whom to share our thoughts and ideas. If we do not have such a friend then what? We often go about looking for friends in the wrong way. Our relationships are selfish without our being conscious of that fact, choosing people who by nature are akin to us and who therefore fall in with our every mood.

Because of the regimentation of modern life (ticket lines, jobs, check-out lines in stores) most of us are forced to associate with those to whom we are not personally attracted. When intimacy with such persons is forced upon us by circumstances, we rebel against it as an intrusion upon our privacy. Our instinct tells us that we have a right to avoid intimacies with all who are unlike us, relationships we did not choose. If we risk giving to unsought relationships, however, we are often surprised at the outcome.

A good friend I have today is one who, as a stranger, stood in line ahead of me at the check-out stand in the grocery store. Circumstances placed us in the same place at the same time. A casual hello evolved into easy conversation. We became best friends. We cannot afford to be selfish in the selection of our friends.

3. *Emotional deprivation.* Paul Tournier writes, "No one comes to know himself through introspection or in the solitude of his personal diary. Rather, it is in dialogue, in his meeting with other persons."[2] We need one person to understand our primary feelings of joy, anger, sadness, and fear.

A best friend is our primary relationship, one we trust most with our feelings. But isn't it unfair to expect one other person to fulfill all our emotional needs? What of days he/she is too busy to listen or too tired or ill? We need more than one friend to share feelings with.

Some of us, more so than others, are intellectual beings. We are not more intelligent than our friends, but we choose to share our thoughts and opinions more than our feelings, perhaps because we are afraid to reveal our feelings.

In some relationships, communication stays on an intellectual plane. Two people share the events of the day but not their feelings in reaction to these events. Conversation is matter-of-fact and "logical." Should they be separated,

2. Paul Tournier, *To Understand Each Other* (Richmond: John Knox Press, 1962), P. 30.

upon reuniting they will politely shake hands and inquire, "How have you been?" Little emotion is shown.

But what happens if one of the two decides that feelings must be shared, too? A common complaint in marriage is, "He/she never shares feelings with me." This is a statement of loneliness and deprivation. Let's cite the example of Karen, who is contemplating leaving John. She insists John "change," meaning that unless John talks more about his feelings, she will leave him. John replies he does not have to change for Karen, that "this is the way I am." He's right. John does not have to share his feelings with Karen unless he chooses. And if he does, it will not be to please Karen or even hold the marriage together but because he senses the excitement of change for himself. "Unless you change" is a form of blackmail, stating if the other person doesn't become what we want him to become, we will abandon him. Karen's options are (1) find a friend with whom to share her feelings, (2) love John for who he is, not what she wants him to become, (3) divorce him.

4. *Spiritual deprivation.* Within organized religion we pursue intimacy with persons who "believe" as we do. Yet, we may be reluctant to share our spiritual fears and doubts, fearing we will appear imperfect. Religion ought never to be *competition in goodness* or outdoing each other in charitable deeds or righteous talk. Competition breeds fear, not compassion.

5. *Physical deprivation.* We need to touch and be touched. Perhaps our need is grounded in childhood when upon incurring a bruise or cut we sought *first* a parent's hug, touch, or kiss.

Our physical and emotional distress is best soothed, I believe, through touching. If we are hospitalized and in pain, a touch, not words, comforts us most. A friend holds our hand or gently strokes our forehead.

Grieving is feeling. What comforts the griever, therefore, is that the listener identifies with *his* feelings. A touch most perfectly embodies the quality of our feelings. Words are symbols, I wrote earlier, that do not adequately express the quality and force of our feelings.

Most of us equate touching with being rocked. Rocking begins in the womb through mother's physical movements. As children we were rocked when held. We do not outgrow our need to rock. For Father's Day one recent year, my wife bought an outdoor swing for two, and I erected it under a tree in our back yard. She and I use it more than the children. Rocking soothes, comforts.

Every home needs a rocking chair for use by children and grownups. The aged, grieving the gradual loss of relationships, friends who die or move away, or death of a mate, derive comfort from rocking. Rocking is, in the absence of another to hold or touch us, a way to comfort ourselves. Water beds undoubtedly are popular for the same reason—rocking comforts.

6. *Sexual deprivation.* Our six needs—presence, emotional, intellectual, physical, spiritual, and sexual—blend.

The question arises, what is sex? Some say sex is the act of intercourse; others feel that if sex is only an act, the emphasis is upon physical performance. Sexual performance, separated from our other needs, can be a lonely experience. Some couples tell me they have "great sex" (physical satisfaction) but communicate poorly outside of the bedroom. If two people rarely touch or share feelings outside of the bedroom, chances are that sex, to them, means the act of intercourse.

A common complaint (women mostly) is that touching outside of the bedroom must always lead to sex. Some of us are conditional touchers; we touch someone with a payoff in mind for ourselves, most often intercourse. Unconditional touching has no payoff. One woman told me, "Sometimes I need a touch more than an orgasm."

Holding someone is a beautiful gift. Our hugs ought not to squeeze the breath out of people. Often, what we are saying when we squeeze hard is, "Please love me."

Hugging is gentle, given with the need of the other in mind. Refrain from patting on the back when hugging. Patting expresses our discomfort or embarrassment, and often signifies, "I've had enough, let's stop."

Sex is not an absolute for it means something different to each of us. Some days sex *will* be a performance, an act. Other days it will be holding someone or simply a "feeling" we cannot explain.

9
What to Do If Grief Grows Morbid

Grief slips into morbidness when we grow preoccupied with thoughts of suicide or talk of nothing other than the loss. There are other signals we should heed: major weight change, insomnia, frequent bursting into tears, social isolation, mounting use of substances (alcohol, drugs), loss of libido (sexual desire), and easy fatigue can signal preoccupation with grief. As a rule, not any *one* signal is too important by itself, but a combination of them should prompt us to seek professional help. Reports Beth, a bank teller grieving loss of her marriage, "One evening I was $900 short in my count and couldn't remember who had come to my window that day. That's when I decided it was time to get professional help." She concluded, "Through counseling I took a disaster and turned it around to work *for* me rather than *against* me."

There are few encounters that two people are more apprehensive about than discussing a loss. Most of the problem lies within friends of the griever who steer clear of grief talk because they are afraid of breaking down themselves. We do not want to burden the griever with our tears or sadness.

But grievers' friends also hesitate to bring up the loss for fear of saying something to cause the griever to break down or "go to pieces." "How would I ever be able to handle that?" is a common question.

Upon losing someone or something important to us, we need to talk immediately of the how, when, and where aspects of the loss. Our minds are foggy after loss. The loss may have occurred before our eyes, but until someone asks us a few pointed questions requiring us to sort the facts, those facts are not clear to us. *Why* questions are not recommended for they encourage philosophizing about the loss. *When, how*, and *where* queries solicit *facts* only. Giving the details to one person is enough. We do not need to repeat them to everyone, a ritual which becomes morbid.

The moment Alice came home from school, her mother detected her sadness. The corners of her mouth drooping, Alice tossed her math book on the kitchen counter, shuffled into the front room, and dropped into a chair. "Why, mom, why does she have to leave?" Upon learning that Alice's favorite teacher had become pregnant and was quitting, mother asked, "Did she announce it to the entire class?" "Yes," Alice responded. Mother then proceeded to elicit further information from Alice: "Did you have any idea she was pregnant?" "Did she say how long she would be out of school?" "When is she quitting?" Giving mother the details clarified the facts in Alice's mind.

One evening when I answered the telephone, I could hear only wailing, punctuated with "no . . . no . . . no." "What has happened?" I asked, recognizing Lynne's voice. "John has just dropped over dead here in the kitchen," she sobbed. Since John was a jogger and supposedly fit at the age of thirty-nine, his death shocked me, but rather than reveal my immediate reaction, I asked for more information on facts of the loss: What time did it happen? What had John been doing when it happened? Had John been sick that day? What had she been doing when it happened? As she gave me the facts her hysteria subsided.

To help someone work through the facts of loss, we should concentrate on the griever's responses, not our own. It comforts the griever to know that we, as friends, also grieve; but frequently we confuse, even anger, the griever with responses such as: "I feel so helpless right now." "I don't know what to say." "I'm at a loss for words."

Raw from the shock of loss, the griever does not want to be told how helpless his/her loss makes friends feel or how uncomfortable or how embarrassed. The griever should not have to expend energy consoling helpless friends. Many grievers choose to carry their feelings silently for this reason. They are not only fearful of making others feel helpless, but bitter that fumbling friends seem to be soliciting their consolation.

In *Widow*, Lynn Caine writes that letters of condolence she received were "expressions of personal awkwardness and discomfort, addressing themselves to the writers distress, not to my sorrow or to our shared loss."[1]

We may choose to write a letter to the griever, stating briefly our prayers and wishes for them, something like "I hope you feel better soon." Comfort lies in knowing someone cares how *we* feel.

But words of condolence, spoken or written, aren't everything. Words can be spun off quickly, and some peo-

1. Lynn Caine, *Widow* (New York: William Morrow and Co., 1974), p 74.

ple who give us their words and expensive cards do not give their time.

Giving our time to the griever is an unconditional gift and the one most often appreciated. We do not give our time out of a sense of duty. Should either of us feel the *need* to talk of the loss, it will occur spontaneously. We do not feel responsible for "doing something" to help the griever talk, nor does the griever feel we are on a mission. The time and mood will feel right.

A traditional offer to the griever is, "If I can be of any help be sure to call." But rarely does the griever do so because he does not want to impose. Rather than say, "Give me a call," it is better to inquire periodically if there is something we can do to help.

The griever can quickly detect the person who *cares* among the people who *pity*. Those who pity often talk down to the griever in a tone of voice reminiscent of a person consoling a two-year-old child who has fallen off his tricycle. You know the tone of voice I am talking about— the "you poor thing" tone.

Another sign of pity is in the answer to the question, "Are we more concerned with the griever's feelings or with our own performance?" Because we dread appearing awkward, we may be overly conscious of our performance, saying the right thing and mustering up a look of concern upon our face that conveys the depth of our sorrow. We may indeed feel sympathy, but the griever is quick to detect our performance. He interprets it as pity for him; the listener is trying too hard.

The person who cares knows when the griever ought to be doing for himself what we are doing for him. If we view the griever as a child, we treat him as a child, insisting he depend upon us. A griever appreciates favors but resents rescuing. Rescuing is manipulating the griever to be dependent upon us.

We do the most for our grieving friends by insisting they, as much as possible, carry on with their normal duties. Rescuing gives us a feeling of importance but insults the griever for it implies he is a helpless child.

Our Need to Remember Loss

With time our loss feelings soften, but we do not forget the actual loss itself.

Some of us feel that bringing up a friend's loss is cruel and that we are being the most helpful by acting as if nothing has happened. But a caring friend senses the value of occasionally bringing up his/her loss.

On Giving Advice

If I believed in absolutes, now would be the time to state one: *Never give advice.*

Advice is an absolute answer whereas a recommendation is an alternative option. A recommendation states, "You could consider such and such an option," then lets the listener decide. But the advice-giver tells us what to do, thus cheating us of the excitement and discipline of choosing our own way.

Of course, small children, too young to understand

danger, need absolutes in the form of limits, so we tell them "If you play in the street, you'll be spanked." And occasionally adults who are critically ill need to be told what to do, as with a doctor who advises hospitalization to one seriously contemplating suicide.

We need to give children *choices within limits* as soon as possible. If, for instance, four-year-old Mary asks her father what dress to wear to the birthday party, he might select three from her closet then suggest Mary pick out the one she wants, thus offering her the fun and discipline of selection. Children grieve loss of the right to choose within limits.

Those of us who give advice to grievers want to be helpful, but in so doing, we fulfill our need to rescue people by discouraging responsibility in them. In addition, giving advice fosters dependency upon us to do the thinking the griever should be doing for himself. Advice is a discount of the griever, saying, "We have the answers, you don't." What's more, if our advice is heeded and then fails, we are blamed for the failure.

Grieving can grow morbid, and we as friends of the griever often feel compelled to say something to prod him into changing his grieving patterns. But what does one say, that's the problem. What do you tell a man, for instance, who has visited the grave of his wife once a day for two years and who talks of little other than that loss? Or what of a teen-ager, Joe, who after moving to a new location, withdraws, refuses to initiate new friendships, loses his appetite, and just broods. We can best help the morbid griever, not by advising what to do but by challenging him, "How long do you think your grief will last?" or "How long do you think it is normal for your grief to go on?" *Let the griever decide what to do.* We cannot talk him out of his feelings, nor can he will his grief away, but he can make decisions to spur the grief process along. In the example of Joe, the grieving teen-ager, angry at his father for uprooting him, I asked, "How long do you feel you will have to stay angry at your dad?" Challenged to decide, he did, first by telling his father how angry he was at him. For Joe this was a big risk for he feared offending his dad. Luckily, his father understood. But in addition to telling him, Joe decided to replace the activity of brooding with new activities. He joined the high school tennis team and drama club. Exchanging activities was anything but easy for Joe. Although a fine tennis player, he went through the motions of tennis at first.

Morbid grievers may have to force, literally drag themselves to replace brooding with a new activity. Sometimes I ask a morbid griever to do some homework, as with a divorcee to whom I said, "Why not sew yourself a dress before our next visit." Prior to her divorce, she loved to sew but lost interest during her grieving period. She did make herself sew a dress, and once she'd completed the project, further sewing grew more natural. But breaking the spell of brooding is hard. In another instance, I suggested to a man, who had grown preoccupied with grief following a move to California from the Midwest, that he write a short story and bring it to me to read. A talented writer, he did, though at first just putting a paragraph together proved to be a major task.

Is brooding or sulking always bad? There is, I believe, a time and place for brooding, *really brooding and sulking*. I learned this from a woman who, grieving loss of her son to college, said that at intervals she "gave in completely" to the sulking temptation by exaggerating her sulking posture. She assumed the sulkiest position she could, slouching deep into a chair, folding her arms across her chest, then crossing her legs with one tucked tightly under the other. And she wailed—oh, did she wail. Other times she exaggerated the despairing look on her face, the deep forehead lines, the drooping corners of her mouth, then told herself out loud how miserable she really felt and that she *deserved* to sulk like this. By occasionally exaggerating her brooding characteristics, the need to brood gradually was dissipated.

One evening, after a lecture I gave on grief, a man strode up to the podium, displayed his bandaged finger, and told of losing its tip in a chain saw accident. "I grieved this loss harder than any loss in my life," he confided, "but my friends don't ask me about it. I wonder if they care." His grief was dual—loss of a finger plus disappointment in friends who seemed not to care enough to bring it up.

When we grieve, our hope is that others will periodically recall our loss, for it proves they have not forgotten and it gives us opportunity to talk of our feelings.

We are, of course, most fearful of initiating dialogue on death loss. In our small midwestern town on a July evening some years ago, the air was humid. I was walking home from the office and observed that people had moved onto their front porches, hoping to catch a vagrant breeze. Striding past a friend's house, I detected soft sobbing. I turned up the walk and entered the porch. As I sat down beside my friend on the swing, I asked her if she was crying over Dan, her late husband. "You are the first one to ask me about him since he died," she said. "You knew him, will you talk about him with me?"

People ask what to do if, after loss, no one brings it up.

105

Others cannot always detect our need to talk, so we sometimes have to take the initiative and request of a friend, "I need to talk about my loss with you now." We are not trained to be that brazen, that "rude," but such boldness is an alternative to simply sitting and feeling sorry for ourselves.

Grief Symbols

Granger Westberg, a pioneer in the field of religion and mental health, notes a period in American history when men mourning a death wore black armbands and grieving women wore a black veil. President Franklin D. Roosevelt, grieving the death of his mother, was the last public figure to wear a black armband. Wearing black had two purposes: It informed people of the loss and gave them permission to ask about it.

Grief symbols—if not black clothing, then a special pin in our lapel or a symbol taped to a window in our hcme or on our car—need resurrecting.

Closure

Each day we feel appreciations and resentments toward people we love. If we express them, we have what is called "closure." If, however, one or both fail to have full daily closure, feelings fester and become unfinished business for the future. Should our friend or relative die before we have a final closure, our grief can be severe. Suddenly, it's too late. What will we do with our feelings now?

The Bible says, "Let not the sun go down on your wrath."

A husband harboring anger toward his wife overnight or longer reveals it in subtle ways like pouting, coming home late for dinner, or lashing out at the children. Unexpressed feelings do not go away.

It is good to mix appreciations and resentments daily. Some of us express only our resentments and withhold our appreciations. "He knows what I appreciate about him, why should I have to tell him?" we often think to ourselves. But our loved ones need to hear appreciations. In fact, everyone does. Unfortunately, many people feel awkward and embarrassed when we try to say something nice. These people should stop to think about the importance of telling their loved ones how much they love and need them. Shared feelings promote more shared feelings—the relationship grows deeper and more rewarding every day.

We cannot, of course, risk closure with everyone. We don't need it with all of our acquaintances, only with those we love most. If we tell our employer how much we resent his turning down our request for a pay raise, we could lose our job. And what of unexpressed resentments toward our parents? Would our resentments be too hurtful, possibly alienate us for good?

There is no absolute rule by which to decide if it is beneficial or destructive to risk closure with aged parents. Every situation differs. Sometimes their reaction surprises us, for they not only listen but say what they themselves have felt for years but never said before.

Children need to hear parents' appreciations — daily. Betty, a woman of fifty-five, states that her father has never hesitated to say what he resents about her, yet he has never told her how he appreciates her. "I've always tried to prove myself to dad. If he would share but a few appreciations of me before he dies, it would do a world of wonder for me," she says.

Marie, a divorcee, grieves loss of closure with her father. An alcoholic and fearful of showing feelings, he wards off Marie's attempts to say what she appreciates and resents about him. She has invited him along with her on country drives and bicycle jaunts, but he responds flatly "no."

Marie feels awkward talking to men today. She traces her awkwardness to childhood and loss of opportunities to "just chat" with her father.

Parents need to give time to their children, during which dialogue can flow naturally and spontaneously. A good way to help children develop confidence in dialogue is joining in their play. Building a sand castle together or playing catch on the driveway creates a relaxed atmosphere in which conversation is easy and relaxed. Children, especially teen-agers, feel awkward and embarrassed going to parents and requesting a rap session over personal problems. The fun of hunting ducks with my father was that it gave us time together to casually banter about a wide variety of subjects, including our relationship. He gave me the gift of *time*.

An alternative to face-to-face closure is writing a letter that states our unfinished business, then mailing it or tearing it up. Sometimes just jotting down our feelings on paper affords us the release we need. Some of my clients choose to send me the letter they have written to aged parents. Talking out our unfinished business with a friend or counselor is another alternative to no closure with someone deceased.

During the two weeks my father lay ill before dying, I told him of appreciations I had felt for years but had kept to myself. I had always assumed he knew I appreciated him. But now, sensing he might not live, I knew I would grieve loss of the opportunity to tell him in person. Still, on the day he died, I felt new appreciations and wrote him a twelve page letter which I still have in my files. Even though my father had died, writing down my feelings gave final closure with him.

Some parents do not allow their children daily closure because it is an affront to their power. When their father promised twins Larry and Barry he would chauffeur them to a tennis tournament 100 miles away but backed down at the last minute, the twins were angry. Their father's reason sounded valid to the twins, but they still needed to express their anger like this: "I'm angry, dad. You got our hopes up and then wham—no trip." Whether or not their father agrees with their anger is not the question. His understanding of their feelings will allow them closure.

Divorce Closure

A twenty-five-year-old marriage, when it does end, ends overnight, which shocks many friends for "they seemed so ideally suited and rarely raised their voices at each other." But like two pressure cookers, when each finally exploded, the unfinished business (unexpressed resentments) swamped the marriage and divorce ensued.

A marriage that ends physically does not end emotionally. So why, if a marriage begins with a ceremony in which two vow faithfulness to each other, should not a shattered marriage end with a ceremony of closure. Few couples who divorce have emotional closure. Instead, unfinished business is channeled through such tactics as withholding support payments, harassment over the telephone, and gossip about the other, all emotionally charged ways of venting unexpressed anger.

The *Sacramento Bee* reported recently that some ministers are conducting a new divorce rite. First an announcement of the dissolution is mailed to friends:

> Neal and Kathy Jones
> announce the dissolution
> of our marriage.
> We ask our friends not
> to take sides and
> to remain friends with
> both of us.
> Kathy will continue
> to reside at 412 Hazel Ave.
> Neal will reside at 611 E. Hamilton.

And then, on a day mutually acceptable, Kathy and Neal kneel in the presence of a minster. Neal begins:

> I have so much hostility toward you, and I feel hurt to the core of my being because of our quarreling the past few months. I still care for you, of course, but I can see our marriage is now one of ugliness and unhappiness.
>
> Now I forgive you for all you have done to me, and I ask your forgiveness for all I have done to you.
>
> And I release you from your marriage vows.

Kathy replies:

Neal, I accept your apology for all that has happened, and I thank you for your forgiveness. I ask you to forgive me also for things I have said.

I release you from your wedding vows, and I ask you to release me from mine.

The minister then gently holds the couple's hands and begins to pray:

God, please guide Neal and Kathy on their way through life from here on. Help them to find the joy you intended. Release them from the hate and hostilities and fill them with your love.

Closure upon divorce would spare husband and wife much grief. It is rarely possible, however. Bitter feelings abound. Individual vulnerability is often nil. I have counseled hundreds contemplating divorce. Some have divorced, others have chosen to set up a new marriage contract. Of those choosing divorce, only several couples have had closure in my office. They, unlike so many today who say "I finally got rid of him/her," have remained friends.

Forgiveness facilitates closure. The word *forgiveness* means "I will not get even with you." Fearful of closure with our loved ones, withholding forgiveness from one requesting it, is a way of "getting even." Look at the example of Ann and her employer. In the wake of a quarrel, Ann, grieving loss of trust between them, returned to his office and requested forgiveness for insulting him. He refused.

She tried again one week later, but he refused again. Ann needs closure, but he gets even by denying her forgiveness.

Getting even is attempting to inflict hurt on someone in return for the way they "hurt us." Ann, stuck in the guilt state of grief, feels desperate and has talked of suicide. Forgiveness heals only after both parties make a *promise*. One requests, "Please forgive me,"; the other responds, "I do," which in essence is promising, "I may have the right to get even but I will not."

Turning Points

How do we know when grief is beginning to soften? There are turning points, and we ought to be aware of them.

Turning points often come when we feel as though we cannot carry on one minute longer. But just as it is darkest before dawn, so our grief seems blackest before it begins to lift.

Somewhere along in the grief cycle everything seems hopeless. We live in a vacuum in which little makes sense, there is nothing to cling to, and we are sure grief will never soften. At times like this, we need to remember that grief is a very predictable form of distress. Eventually it always softens. Talking to someone who has "made it" through grief gives us the hope we will "make it" too.

Donna, following loss of a love affair, worked through the main body of grief in six months, during which she dropped out of her bowling league. She stayed home evenings and did not initiate any social contacts. Concerned friends called to invite her along on outings, but Donna gave excuses to stay home. Near the end of six months, Donna's best friend, Anne, called one evening. Here is part of their conversation:

ANNE: How are you, dear?
DONNA: I've had a good week, Anne. For some reason I feel like getting out more. Last night I surprised myself by going to a movie.
ANNE: It sounds like you are feeling better. One reason I'm calling is to remind you that bowling is tomorrow night. We haven't forgotten about you, you know.
DONNA: That sounds pretty good to me. I might just start up again. I've been cooped up in this house about long enough.

Donna was showing interest in an old activity again, and this was a turning point for her. She returned gradually to her other interests: gardening and skiing. In addition she bought a new suit and a new plant for her house. When Donna took a short holiday, friends knew her grief was softening.

Grief, then, has turning points. They come naturally, and as they do, we take heart: Our grief is softening.

10
Loss Is Relative

One evening during dinner my youngest daughter placed a glass of milk in front of me, asking, "Is it half full or half empty, dad?" Amused at my reluctance to answer she chuckled, "It's what you want it to be, half full or half empty."

She's right. That milk glass, as with life itself, is what we want it to be. We can choose to be gloomy or hopeful, optimistic or pessimistic.

We cannot control what happens to us, but we are responsible for our reaction to everything that happens to us. When Bill and Margaret arrived home from a bridge party, they were shocked to discover that a burglar had broken into the house and stolen a treasured silverware gift. They could not prevent this loss. Nor could they ward off their grief reaction. But they are responsible for the *outcome of their grief*.

Following a loss we cannot control feelings that arise within us. They flow from deep within. But we can choose our attitude toward grief. We can value our feelings or despise them. It is up to us. Fourteen personal qualities shape our reaction to change.

1. Familial grief patterns. A family hands down grief patterns and rituals from one generation to the next. Children learn "how to" grieve from mother and father. Most influential upon children, however, is not what parents say about loss but how they themselves react to loss.

Should children be allowed to see parents grieve? What, for instance, of the grieving father who releases grief feelings only when alone in his car or working in the garden? Parents who *intentionally* hide grief feelings from children do them a disfavor, for then children do not receive permission to openly grieve loss. They conclude that grief denial is a test of "strong" character.

After our family moved from a Minnesota village to a Wisconsin city, my father, I recall, grieved off and on for weeks, neither withdrawing into solitude nor explaining his grief. Observing him sad or tearful, I received permission to reveal my grief over that same loss.

By their example, parents teach children that winning means glory and that losing is weakness or even disgrace. Let's cite the example of Mary, who after a spirited Ping Pong game in which she nips her father by one point watches him stalk angrily away. Next time, to stay on the good side of him, she may decide to lose. That way he will not be angry with her.

Children competing in athletics, though giving their best to the game, need to occasionally lose to learn they cannot *always* win and that loss is natural to life.

2. Body image and grief. To each part of our body, an external limb or an internal organ, we assign a value. We value some bodily parts moreso than others, placing a higher worth, say, upon our legs than upon our hearing. If we lose a leg, then, we will grieve that loss more intensely than if we lose our hearing.

Body image is the picture we form in our minds of our bodies. Am I ugly or pretty? Some people who are physically attractive to others have a personal body image of ugliness, wearing clothes and makeup to camouflage their "ugly" parts. One of my clients was born with a blue eye and a brown eye, though the difference cannot be detected unless one stands close to her. Friends think she is attractive and tell her so. But the mental picture she carries of her face is, "I am ugly." She wears tinted glasses to "hide the handicap." She refuses party invitations, living the life of a near recluse.

Parents' attitudes toward parts of their bodies—sexual organs especially—are imparted to children, making a deep impression upon the child's concept of his body.

Bob recalls growing up in a home where mother undressed for bed every night in a dark closet. He concluded that the naked body was ugly. He suffers from impotency in his marriage.

Our body concept is often drastically altered following the amputation of a limb, called the phantom limb phenomenon. The phantom limb is a physical sensation associated with the lost extremity, as in the stump that remains.

Bernard Schoenberg and Arthur Carr, pioneers in studying the relationship of grief to loss of body parts, say that the phantom limb phenomenon "may be noted after sudden change in body size such as that which occurs following childbirth."[1]

1. Bernard Schoenberg et al, eds., *Loss and Grief, Psychological Management in Medical Practice* (New York and London: Columbia University Press, 1970), p. 121.

As to recovery from the phantom limb grief symptom, they go on to say: "The sensations may be tingling, pins and needles, or disagreeably painful sensations, and with some patients the total disappearance may take as long as several years. It is of interest that children who have amputations before the age of six or seven, or children who are born without limbs, do not experience the phantom phenomena."[2]

Patients often fantasize what is done with the severed limb, feeling the sensation of burning pain. "I have heard what happens to organs that are removed. I know they are put in the incinerator and burned."[3]

The ritual of saving severed limbs until the victim died, then burying them with the rest of the body, was introduced first into China by medical missionaries. In fact, the Chinese would not allow doctors to amputate until after receiving assurance that the limb would be saved. The Orthodox Jews have continued this practice up to the present day. The Talmud states that the heart, kidneys, and other organs necessary to sustain life shall be buried with the rest of the body.

Schoenberg and Carr concluded that we should not be shocked that an individual might want a prized or loved part of himself to be disposed of with dignity and that it is natural to want to know the whereabouts of our body parts.

An illustration of this is Willie in Carson McCullers's *The Heart is a Lonely Hunter*, who has lost both his legs.

I feel like my feets is still hurting. I got this terrible misery down here in my toes. Yet the hurt in my feets

2. Ibid.
3. Ibid.

is down where my feets should be if they were on my l-l-legs. And not where my feets is now. It is a hard thing to understand. My feets hurt me so bad all the time and I don't know where they is. They never given them back to me. They s-somewhere more than a hundred m-miles from here. . . . I just wish I know where my feets are. That the main thing worries me. The doctors never given them back to me. I sure do wish I knowed where they are.

Do you remember losing your first tooth and what you did with it? I hid mine under the pillow to collect the tooth fairy's reward. Then I put it in a box to keep in my dresser drawer. That tooth was the very first part of ME that I lost. I wanted to save it.

Or take the example of a mother who saves the first lock of hair shorn from her child's head, pressing the hair between book leaves or putting it in an envelope.

Some even choose to save extracted body parts. While I was visiting in the home of new friends one day, my eye fell upon a small bottle atop a mantelpiece over the fireplace. Upon strolling over to get a better look at its contents, I saw that the bottle contained gallstones, thirty in all. My hostess seemed immensely pleased that I should show such interest in this "lost" part of her. The fact is, those stones would probably never be lost.

The mere thought of cremating a deceased loved one repels some of us. The loss would be too absolute. We need to bury the body so we can visit the remains. As we stand over the grave our grief is soothed. We feel a presence, a nearness. Even though our reason tells us the loved one is gone, we need to *feel* a link with him.

Besides its physical usefulness, a limb's value is ascertained by its physical attractiveness and symbolism. An example is the female breast—an object of admiration if not worship by many males and set forth in movies as *the* symbol of femininity and sexuality. A woman whose desireability resides mainly in her size 38 bustline may severely grieve the removal of a cancerous breast. Many women report that loss comparable to the death of a loved one.

A small-breasted woman whose shapely body draws ogling and whistling from males will probably not grieve as heavily should she one day need a mastectomy.

A hysterectomy (females) and vasectomy (males) can initiate heavy grief. Some men become impotent after a vasectomy over "loss" of their sexual identity. Some women, in turn, grieve a hysterectomy, for it dashes their dreams of bearing children.

We cannot escape forming a mental picture of our appearance, but it ought not to be the chief reason we value ourselves. Feeling loved (or rejected) based on appearance alone is frightening, for should a burn or scar alter our appearance what will there be about us to love?

Over the years I have counseled many physically attractive women who grieve loss of unconditional love. They feel valued for their splendid appearance and resent people who don't value their inner qualities. One such grieving woman is Eve, a stunning blond (my perception of her appearance), tall and poised as she swept into my office. She began, "Men see me as a challenge, someone to pursue, to win, and when I show interest in one, he often stops calling. I want to be valued for me, not for just a pretty face." Down through the years, she had won six beauty contests but was fed up with them; she was lonely and afraid of people.

I suggested she join my treatment group, which she did. There she began unveiling her fears and mistrust, her attempts to live up to the image others held of her, spending large sums on clothes, devoting several hours daily to applying makeup and tending her hair. Group members listened without judgment, valuing all her feelings. A turning point came the evening she strolled into group dressed in sloppy jeans and with her hair rolled up in curlers. Eve was beginning to trust group members who loved her for *who* she was, not her appearance. Old friends who valued Eve to feed *their* egos began to drop away. Eve formed new friendships based upon an appreciation of her personal qualities, not her beauty alone.

Here is a helpful exercise to determine the mental image you hold of your face. Look at your face in a mirror three times daily for the next month, repeating each time, "I love you." What do you feel when you say the words? Disgust? Warmth? If you are a male, can you say at 7:00 A.M.— whiskers and hair disheveled—"I love you"? And women, can you love your face without makeup?

An excellent group exercise goes like this. Ask for a volunteer. Say that Gloria raises her hand. Give her a mirror and request she study her face in the mirror. As she does, ask for several people to assemble behind her and also observe Gloria's face in the mirror. Ask Gloria to say what she sees in her face, using "I see" phrases. When Gloria stops, group members give their observations, using "I see" sentences. For people such as Gloria, this is often the first time they actually hear others value their face for some quality other than a well-shaped nose, an olive complexion, or attractive eyes. They hear instead character words like *kindness, sensitivity,* and *understanding,* or *fear, anxiety.*

Do Women Grieve More Thoroughly than Men?

The criticism that men do not feel as deeply as women is simply not true. What is true is that men are every bit as feeling as women though men do not always divulge feelings as easily. Reason: Little boys are taught that men do not cry or that little boys who do cry are weak.

I am against any absolute statement portraying women as possessing one quality and men another. Men tolerate physical pain as well as women, and men are as loving as women.

Male and female, though equal, are not the same sexually. Nor do females possess the brute strength of men. But little girls, given the opportunity to wrestle and play football, would develop the brute strength boys do.

During a big league baseball game I attended, the batter was struck on the upper left arm by a blazing fast ball. He hardly flinched, sprinting down to first base as if nothing had happened. His arm, I'm sure, throbbed plenty; but he chose to hide the pain from the crowd; the "mark," it seems, of a courageous athlete. It's true that some men believe that revealing feelings is a weakness, but such a notion stems from cultural training and is not an innate quality that all males possess and all females do not.

Do women grieve more thoroughly than men? There is no absolute answer. Adult enrollment in the loneliness course I teach averages nine women for every man. My overall conclusion is that men *tend* to avoid subjects focusing on feeling.

3. Self-image and grief. What we expect to receive from life—happiness or misery, success or failure—is called self-image.

People fail for two reasons: Some of us are overconfident—the talented swimmer, for instance, who, careless in training, makes a poor showing at the regional meet. But far more of us fail because we lack confidence, do not think highly enough of ourselves.

Deserving to fail or "lose," we set on a course to prove it, manipulating people and events in order to hold them responsible for our losses. But then our grief is unnatural and contrived. We have a *need* to lose.

We smile sometimes at how children attempt to manipulate others. Here is a typical manipulative transaction between a mother and her seven-year-old daughter, Sandy.

THE SCENE: Sandy has just burned her fingers on a hot pan that is standing on the stove. Sandy yelps, bringing mother into the kitchen.

MOTHER: What in the world has happened?

SANDY: My fingers, my fingers, you look at them, I can't because I'll pass out.

MOTHER: Here, let me put some ice cubes on them.

SANDY: (after mother has applied ice) Mother, if you would just be more careful about taking hot pans off the stove this wouldn't have happened.

Sandy's charge is true. If mother had removed the pan Sandy wouldn't have burned her fingers. That, however, is not the point. The thing is, Sandy attempted to place the sole blame on mother to avoid responsibility for her own actions.

Blaming others, we achieve our goal of helplessness. Twenty-eight-year-old Carol is what is commonly called a loser. Because of her low self-esteem, she solicits rejection. She initiates conversations with hooking statements such as: "Guess what happened to me *this* week." "You'll never believe this one." "Boy, have I got a dilly for you."

She unconsciously wants retorts such as: "Poor thing." "Why don't you start to shape up some?" "You certainly do have a lot of bad luck, don't you?"

Carol attempts to manipulate a negative response from others to *feel* a loser.

We may even read the Bible to confirm our loser image, concentrating on verses that condemn us and intentionally skipping over verses on love and forgiveness. I have seen Bibles in which the reader underlined in red ink every verse describing the wages of sin and the ravages of hell.

Feeling manipulated by people such as Carol, we may choose three forms of response. We can ignore manipulative statements. Here ignoring does not mean ignoring the person. Rather we change the subject or in some other way avoid giving the needed response. The manipulator could take silence as meaning, "You don't care enough about me to answer." But a response other than the expected one will at least surprise the manipulator, and it might make him aware that we are tired of playing his game.

Secondly, we may choose to agree with the manipulative statements, or thirdly, we may risk our honest reaction, saying, "I feel manipulated and do not like the feeling. Can't we do something other than talk about your misfortunes?"

In so saying, we assume the responsibility for our own reaction. In Carol's case, friends do occasionally risk saying, "I'm feeling manipulated." But Carol doesn't listen, for she has not yet decided to begin liking herself. To begin with she will have to replace old ways of passing time (talking about her tribulations) with new rituals, like a hobby. If we have felt the need to lose, feeling good about ourselves frightens us at first. Good feelings are alien to us. We do not trust them. A friend will need to reassure us that liking ourselves is perfectly all right.

Roles and Loss

Nan was raised to be dependent. Growing up, she was known in the community as a professor's *daughter*, later when she married, as a doctor's *wife*, and finally, as the *mother* of three children. The role of doctor's wife earned her special favors and lots of social status, but her divorce ended all that. Though she was still a mother, that single role did not provide her with sufficient identity strength. She recalls, "I did not know who I was anymore. Overnight I became a nobody." From childhood, Nan's life centered on fulfilling the expectations and responsibility of roles. Not having tested the personal qualities that make Nan the unique person she is, when these roles were stripped away, Nan was a stranger to herself. With the aid of professional help, she is establishing her own identity. Living exclusively in a role influences our reaction to change.

Lynn Caine, grieving loss of her husband writes:

Women, understandably, were the most sympathetic and perceptive, but many men wrote sensitive letters too. It is sad that the progression of grief is so much more difficult for widows than widowers. But there is a reason for it. Men do not think of themselves as husbands and fathers. They have been encouraged to develop their full potential as human beings. So when a man becomes a widower it is truly a heartbreaking blow, but it does not spell an end to his whole way of life. He still has his identity, one that has developed through work, through play, through living.[4]

Dreams and Grief

Unresolved grief feelings often make themselves known through bad dreams or nightmares. Besides robbing us of sleep, nightmares may prompt the panic that we are finally losing our minds, just as we dreaded we might. Not only are we preoccupied with our loss feelings all day long, but we dream about them at night, too. Is there no relief?

Grief dreams should not be shrugged off. If we keep a pad of paper by our bed and, upon awakening, write down as many details of our nightmare as we can recall, we can think them through later and perhaps learn more about our grief. We may even seek the dream interpretation from a professional or from a book such as Ann Faraday's *Grief and Dreams*.

4. Lynn Caine, *Widow* (New York: William Morrow and Co., 1974), p. 176.

We don't feel the same degree of grief over the loss of every person or every object because grief is relative. Our grief is in proportion to the time, love, and money we invested in the lost person, place, pet, or object. For Jack, a traumatic grief reaction set in after his decision to sell the old family cabin, a gathering place of three generations spanning sixty years. He spent each boyhood summer there, collecting his fondest memories. Jack had good reasons to sell the place, for its timbers were rotting and he lacked the money to make repairs. Yet, when Jack signed the deed over to the new owner, grief came. Here is the sequence of his grief.

Shock. Although Jack decided to sell two months prior to the actual sales transaction, he felt vague shock when the day arrived. "I couldn't believe I was going through with it," he said. "It seemed to be a dream."

Sobbing. The day after the sale, Jack sobbed. "A part of me seemed to be torn away," he explained. Jack recounted that since childhood he had moved fifteen times. The family cabin had been the one permanent fixture in his transient life, a place he could "be sure of." Giving it up was giving up a part of *himself*.

Physical symptoms. For a week Jack had no appetite and he slept poorly.

Guilt. This was Jack's most excruciating stage of grief. For weeks gnawing doubts plagued him, for he wondered if he had "done the right thing."

Anger. Jack's anger was directed mainly at himself, although he also blamed his wife, of whom he said, "She put pressure on me to sell."

Relief. Having worked through anger, Jack became

aware of relief. He would not have to make cabin repairs or dole out hefty sums for cabin taxes.

Limbo. His grief softened slowly. Has he gotten over that loss? As Jack himself put it, "As long as I live I will probably grieve from time to time, even though I chose to give the place up."

As with any loss, grief does not melt away, never to return. Grief softens. A scar remains.

Dependence and Loss

"Our friends," said Emerson with characteristic insight, "are those who make us do what we can." Friendship is most helpful to others not when it makes things easy for them but when it inspires the best in them, not smoothing over their failures and mistakes but insisting they become responsible in every way. No healthy nature is willing to allow a parasite relationship; a healthy nature demands health in others. In friendship there must be equality between the friends so that each gives and takes. There are limits beyond which even friendship cannot go; when it does it grows morbid and debilitating to both the parasite and the one who supports him.

A parasite relationship discourages responsibility. The one who carries the responsibility of the relationship derives a feeling of power and false importance; the one who leeches off the other is encouraged to feel helpless and dependent. Upon the loss of the friendship, the helpless one will grieve his helplessness and the supporting one his need to be supportive.

The Timeliness of Loss

There is no right time, no best time for loss. Some losses are linked to our age: Acne is linked to the teen years, and our hearing is most apt to degenerate beginning in the fifties and sixties.

We observe of one who has died, "It was his time." Yet, any person who loves life does not want to die—ever. There are always new corners of the globe to explore, new relationships to form, new goals to attain. My grandfather at age ninety-six said, "I would like to write one more book before I die." He passed away shortly after that, but had he attained 150 years he would not have reached every goal he set.

We mourn the timing of loss. Catcher Roy Campanella, at the zenith of a brilliant career, was paralyzed from the neck down in a violent car accident. Baseball fans mourned the loss of a rare baseball talent and the timing of the loss, for Campy could have had many baseball years left. Confined to a wheelchair today, Campanella works with youth, his courageous example an inspiration to them.

Our bias that loss is less fair to children than to the elderly is not always true. We grieve a child's death because he had so much of life yet to live and we wonder what he could have become. But losing a lifelong marriage partner can be equally grievous. Elmer and Louise were married forty-five years. A rural mail carrier, Elmer meticulously saved a portion of his salary each month for a trip they planned to take around the world after his retirement. Seven days before Elmer made his last mail run Louise died. To him Louise's death seemed so "unfair," the timing so cruel.

Piggyback Losses

Grieving consumes our energy. We need adequate time between losses to grieve. If we are cheated of that time, loss feelings can grow entangled. Joe's wife of seventeen years decided to end the marriage. After the shock and sobbing stages, Joe moved into the guilt stage of grief. Feeling he had "taken her for granted," Joe embarked on a zealous campaign to woo her back with love notes and floral bouquets. In the midst of this grief, Joe's boss summoned him into the office to tell him he had been demoted for "falling down on the job." Joe plunged back into the shock stage in response to his new loss. His appetite dwindled, his resistance to disease weakened, and he developed a lung infection that put him in the hospital. Joe needed two things now: medicine to heal the infection and professional counseling to help him work through the grief of two major losses.

When counseling divorced persons (many of whom have temporarily lost trust in the opposite sex), I caution against risking future commitment too soon. To work through the grief of a loss we need ample time before undertaking another commitment.

Children who grieve their parents' divorce should not be hurried through grief by an anxious parent who has decided to remarry. The child may still be working through his loss feelings over the divorce. A divorced father who is in love again invites resentment from the child when he pleads, "Please try to like Kim," referring to his new love. Given time the child may grow to like Kim, but his loss feelings must soften first.

Neither should a child be commanded by a divorced mother, "Don't be angry with your father!" A grieving child *does* blame one parent or the other for the divorce, and sometimes that blame borders on hate. Rather than command the child *how* to feel, parents should listen to any feelings he might express. Asking a child to pretend teaches him to deny his authentic feelings.

> JOSHUA: Mom, I really hate dad for leaving you.
> MOTHER: Josh, I don't like to hear you talk that way about your father. He loves you and wants the best for you. You *should* show appreciation, not anger.

Josh will either flare up at his mother or stop talking. Either way, he will feel misunderstood.

The same situation can be handled in a more constructive manner:

> JOSHUA: I'll never be able to forgive dad for leaving you for another woman. I hate him for the way he's treated you.
> MOTHER: It makes you angry that dad could do something like this.
> JOSHUA: Right, mom. I really don't care if I ever see him again. I just want him to stay out of my life from here on in.
> MOTHER: You're so angry that you don't even want him to set foot in the house.

Mother, though hurt at being abandoned by her husband, may not completely agree with Joshua's judgment of his father. But if she understands his anger, it will soften. Joshua's trust in his mother will grow, too.

When to Risk New Relationships

Those of us who own a compass know that a metal object close by throws the compass needle off. There is an old saying, "Protect your compass from personal deflection." Personal judgment, like the compass, can be deflected. A headache, a gloomy day, lack of sleep, or a quarrel can cloud our judgment.

Choosing is risking. The outcome of our choices cannot be predicted. Sometimes we win; other times we lose. Choosing when our judgment is deflected is irresponsible, for we know in advance that we cannot be responsible for failure and grief. Wisdom dictates we wait before choosing.

Aging and Grief

Whoever said that life begins at fifty was not suggesting that aging is all loss or all gain. The book of Ecclesiastes reads, "There is a time to laugh and a time to mourn." Aging is a combination of both. Whether we find more to laugh about than to mourn depends upon our attitude toward aging.

Life events remind us we are aging. Some adults, when informed they will soon become grandparents, have mixed feelings. They are joyous, of course; but they also grieve. Grandparenthood is one more reminder of aging. One grandfather-to-be described it this way: "What hurts most is that I will be living with a grandmother!"

Aging is a process in which we grieve our own impending death. Each quarter I receive my alma mater *Alumnus* magazine. Of late each issue records an upswing in the death rate of my old college friends. Their passing seems impossible, for "only yesterday" we joked together and shared our dreams. I grieve each death. In addition, each death reminds me of my own impending death. I am not morbid; I do not dwell on it. But I am reminded more often these days, and it strengthens my resolve to value the time and relationships I have now.

Physical losses also remind us of our age. We spot our first gray hairs. We start wearing bifocals. We notice stiffness in our joints. To some people, these are little griefs, but to others they are big griefs. Some can accept aging while others cannot—a man may bleach his graying hair to look younger and a woman may have a face-lift.

Snaillike erosion of our usefulness to society is another reminder. Work experience suddenly seems to take second place to the vitality of youth. A brilliant man with thirty years' experience, now unemployed, is unable to find a job because, at age fifty-six, he is "over the hill." Grieving silently, he has suffered one heart attack and developed migraine headaches.

In middle life, a major loss is often the loss of "those old romantic feelings." A new trend, the twenty-year itch, has recently arisen: The divorce rate among couples married twenty years or more is on the rise. One big reason for the rising divorce rate is the loss of mutual goals surrounding children's needs. Conversations, plans, and trips always included the children. Each time one of them graduated from high school and left home, a void was created. If during the child-raising years the mother and father have not taken the time to communicate with each other or do things independently of the children, they will be strangers to each other when the last child leaves home.

The twenty-year itch is often caused by grief over the loss of those tingly feelings that permeated courtship. We fantasize that romance can be recaptured with someone new. An affair that is motivated by grief over loss feelings, however, cannot last long. Meeting a lover in a hotel room may set one's heart a-pounding for a few minutes, but it is a static moment—one detached from all other time and reality. There is no shared financial commitment, no shared joy or sorrow, no shared feelings of compromise hammered out through painful give and take. Parents who have shared highs and lows acquire a long view of their marriage which lends understanding and trust to the present.

Does an affair ever enhance a marriage? The rule of thumb is that an affair may satisfy the curiosity of the one seeking the affair, particularly his need to explore long-held sexual fantasies. What that satisfaction adds to the marriage is hard to predict. It may, through comparison, aggravate discontent, or it may prompt a decision to redouble efforts to solve problems within the marriage.

The following is a conversation between two friends, Ray and Len, over an affair Len is having:

RAY: Rumor has it that you and Marie are on the verge of splitting up. Someone told me they saw you with another woman the other night.

LEN: You're right on both counts. There is another woman.

RAY: After eighteen years of marriage, you're thinking of breaking it up. That's a heck of a big investment.

LEN: The last year or so we haven't had much to talk about. Marie just doesn't excite me anymore.

RAY: The new woman does?

LEN: Ray, I've never felt this way before about any woman, even my first love in high school. Marie just doesn't hold a candle to Carol.

RAY: Tell me more.

LEN: For one thing, Carol shares her feelings and Marie doesn't. Carol is an outdoor person like me. I'm getting tired of Marie's ideas of fun—things like bridge and having people over for dinner.

By comparing his wife to his new lover, Len is discounting Marie's uniqueness and dodging commitment to problem solving within the marriage. Comparing is a poor basis for responsible choosing. We have qualities that make us unique. If, after counseling, two decide their differences are beyond mediation, it is best to dissolve the marriage and *then* strike out in search of someone new.

I have always liked Saint-Exupéry's line, "Love does not consist in gazing at each other but in looking outward in the same direction." Gazing but at each other, our relationship grows self-centered and dwells on our feelings. But feelings, like quicksand, shift. Trusting them as the foundation for love is precarious.

Expectations and Loss

For sheer delight few events in life surpass planning a honeymoon. A couple charts the honeymoon, fantasizes the first "glorious" days of married life together. But what happens? There are good times, true, but they rarely match expectations: It may rain for four straight days, the car breaks down in the middle of nowhere, and sex? Well, it just wasn't what each thought it would be.

The reason most teen marriages fail is lost expectations. Teenagers in love with glowing fantasies of love and marriage can mistake them for reality. The teen years ought to be a time in life when fantasy roams freely, when dreams of the perfect marriage abound. But carrying grandiose fantasies into marriage sets us up for disappointment. We may seek to reform our mate to match our fantasies, or we may grieve the gradual loss of our fantasies; either course of action is likely to end in divorce. To succeed in marriage, we must work to accept our mate unconditionally (Yes, marriage is hard work).

Vacations, holidays, and birthdays are times when expectations often soar unrealistically and become occasions for grieving loss of those expectations.

There is a place in *The Bacchantes* where Euripides exclaims, "If man, in his brief moment goes after things too great for him he may lose the joys within his reach." These days we are in frantic pursuit of fun. Not only do we have to "go somewhere" to have fun but we're also convinced the further we go from home the more fun we'll have.

The pursuit of fun is turning into an ordeal, throwing many of us into grief over smashed expectations.

Dan, forty-five, married, the father of four, is among the throng of Americans who structure their lives around two quite special days, Saturday and Sunday, resolving, "I am going to have fun this weekend even if it kills me." It does. Traveling and exercise, enough for one week, are squeezed into two days. Activity is furious. Monday morning, worked to a frazzle, he complains of needing a day in bed to rest up.

Every Monday morning, year around, a small army of embattled weekend warriors crawls into orthopedic offices across the land. They come in from ski slopes, water-skiing mishaps, motorbike spills in the forest, with an assortment of dislocations, sprains, and wrenched and pulled muscles. Summer, winter, fall, or spring, it makes little difference.

Why do we travel everywhere under the sun in search of "fun?" Our glittering expectations of that fun rarely materialize. Fun may be elsewhere, but we miss out on so much fun right where we are, often within a one-block radius of home, and it is free of the price of admission.

In fact, to understand the reasons for our costly pursuit of fun, we must first look closely at children's play. The years one through ten embrace innocence, wonder, and imagination. Before fourth grade the little person calls fun what it feels like: play. "Can you come out and play?" he invites another friend, or later on, when permission is needed, "Will your mother let you come out and play?" That invitation to explore together is, I believe, the most beautiful of all children's expressions.

In middle life we complicate elementary virtues; innocence and a sense of wonder stagger under the weight of heavy responsibility and career sophistication. "The hardest people to entertain are the middle-age," a circus clown told me. "I don't see them laugh much. The reason must be all of the responsibility they carry—car payments, child raising. Middle-age people don't smile like children or older folks."

The middle years are supposed to be our most productive years, the time we "leave our mark" in life. So seeing a child swinging on a gate we say, "Go find something to do," forgetting that the child is doing something—swinging on a gate. Invariably, when we grow up, instead of swinging on gates when we feel like it, we go out and find something constructive to do.

The long weekend is here, you can do anything you want. Do you lie in the hammock in the backyard and read a book? No. Instead you make up a list of little jobs you've been putting off doing for six months and spend your day doing what you should do rather than what you *want* to do. One reason: The model citizen in our culture is the person who not only works all day but helps with the Sunday school and Boy Scouts and somehow also manages to keep his roses pruned and lawn from being taken over by crabgrass. Ogden Nash once wrote that most people suffer from "hardening of the oughteries." We feel we ought to do this, ought to do that, ought to be perfect. But inside we hate those oughts.

Eileen Peck, writing in *The Baby Trap*, says: "We prefer not to spend money on possessions and status and gadgetry, rather on experiences and sensations." To children, play is sensations. It is innocence when a child, such as I saw one day, swats wildly at specks of dust that hang suspended in a shaft of sunlight. Grinning, he watched them skittering wildly until the sun caught the branch of a maple tree outside the window and gobbled up his magic. A child delights in simple things. To help you remember how it was, write down twenty-five things you did for fun as a kid—anything at all—like eating watermelon on top of the water tower at midnight or jumping into piles of autumn leaves. Weren't most of them free of the price of admission and were they further than three or four blocks from home? Here's some of my list.

Floating down the river on a homemade raft
Going up the down escalator
Playing on a lumber pile
Eating green apples with salt
Climbing a windmill
Marching in a parade
Picking a wishbone
Following a cow trail on a hillside
Walking to the top of a hill at sunset

The value of play lies in the spirit, the effort, not the outcome. Billy hears parents say, "We've got to make the most of this weekend," and he scratches his head, bewildered.

Child play has no goals: winning, deadlines, weight loss, and toned-up muscles are unimportant. The present counts for everything. Writing about her childhood in *We Took to the Woods*, Louise Dickinson Rich recalls: "A hole in the ground among the roots of a maple tree that grew in front of our house. It was moist and smelled of earth and water when I lay on my stomach and thrust my four year old face into it. It was everything that was marvelous and mysterious to me then and somehow it still is."

Vacations Are Overrated

The value of long vacations, three or four weeks as far from home as possible, has always been overrated.

What happens? A family living together for fifty weeks out of the year has tensions, but they also have safety valves for tension through individual exercise and periodic solitude. In the car and off to "elsewhere," the family, crammed into the car all day, will not have outlets for tension unless stops are frequent. Pressure to "get there" has ruined more than one cross-country trip.

Long vacations fail for another reason: barking dogs in the back seat, no games to play or books to read in the car, and spending the entire vacation visiting in-laws. In-laws, no matter how much we love them, should be invited to visit on nonvacation days.

If you elect to try a vacation at home here are some hints: (1) Do things you have never done before. A vacation is most beneficial if it is away from usual routine and compulsive habits. (2) Forget housework. If you are making home your headquarters taking short jaunts here and there and if the house must be tidy, hire someone to come in to do the dusting. (3) Take the phone off the hook. (4) Eat as many meals out as you can afford.

A Sense of Humor Helps

A cardinal determinant of grief is our willingness to poke playful fun at ourselves. The man who parades his triumphs is a bore; the man who likes himself enough to occasionally laugh at his mistakes and losses is fun. Possessing a sense of humor serves to make us more pliable toward daily change and provides us a release for our grief energy.

Bob Hope, poking fun at himself, once said, "I did some boxing in my younger days, you know. I was the only fighter in Cleveland who fought with a rearview mirror. I was also the only fighter who had to be carried both ways—into the ring and out of it."

What is so funny about self-directed humor? There is a touch of cowardice in us all, and it is reassuring to hear someone human enough to laugh at himself.

If you have lived in a small town, you may have read the local newspaper, the backbone of any small community and the Bible to many. Most of the news items are written by inexperienced but faithful correspondents. Recently, one small-town paper chronicled its "bloopers," poking fun at itself. Among them:

> This being Easter Sunday, we will ask Mrs. Smith to come forward and lay an egg on the altar.

> This afternoon there will be a meeting in the north and south ends of the church. Children will be baptized at both ends.

> Thursday at 8:00 P.M. there will be a meeting of the Little Mothers' club. All those wishing to become Little Mothers please meet with the minister in his study.

Some days we simply cannot laugh in response to anything that happens to us; nothing about change is funny. But other days, the ability to laugh keeps alive our sense of humor in reaction to change. No loss, regardless of its severity, ought to drown our sense of humor. At one time in American history laughing-gas parties were popular. People would inhale this gas (nitrous oxide) and spend the evening laughing at others and at themselves. The reason for laughing was not important. What counted was the therapeutic value of the laugh.

Sentiments and Loss

If we focus exclusively on the "good old days" we are unwilling to evaluate new ideas and philosophies. Resisting change, we grieve all change as loss.

During the years I was a clergyman, one family criticized everything I did, lauding the minister and church "back home" in Missouri as the "best." After I moved to a new church, who should show up but this same family, prodding my memory with "remember when?" They were, I concluded, among those for whom the past is always best because it is the *past*. They did not have permission to think or evaluate change.

Seasons and Grief

Spring is the time of year when everything in nature is menthol fresh. Most suicides occur in May, for if we are grieving, the contrast between our misery and new life in nature drives us to despair. In short, the gap between what we feel and what we want to feel becomes intolerable.

During any month of the year many of us dread changing locations but for one living in New Hampshire and moving to Florida, October is the worst time, for we grieve leaving the fall colors, the smell of damp leaves. Or moving just before Christmas, a season of rituals surrounding long-standing friends and relatives.

Summarily, we should never judge the quality of another's grief by comparing theirs to ours. We grieve uniquely. To call someone odd or calloused who does not show grief like ours over a similar loss, is unfair to them, a judgment discounting the uniqueness of their grieving experience.

11
Religion and Loss

I do not want to present a case for or against religion. But I do want to suggest that faith, whatever form it takes, influences our reaction to change.

Religious faith offers guidelines to help evaluate the worth of people and things, but it ought not to make our reactions and attitudes absolute. During boyhood I had the prejudice that *all* Protestants were good people and going to heaven whereas *all* Catholics were bad and going to hell. There were no exceptions. It was black and white. Of course, now I know that religious faith, unlike marks given in school, cannot be graded.

Grieving intensely is no more an indication of a "weak" faith than is grieving lightly a proof of a "strong" faith. Many believers actually deny their grief reaction, believing God loves them only when they are nice or joyful. The Corrigans, Tim and Jan, childless, took a foster child into their home, "after giving the decision over to God." Four years passed and then the natural mother requested her son back. The Corrigans, wearing polite smiles, complied, rationalizing this change as God's will; all gain and no loss.

Whatever God's will is, they agreed, must be all gain. But Jan developed migraine headaches, a physical symptom of denying anger over the loss. When she understood why she was angry, Jan could talk her feelings through and her grief softened.

I encourage grieving people who are angry at God to write him a letter telling him exactly how they feel, with no holds barred. Here is the portion of the letter one man wrote after learning his son was born blind.

God, you seem very far from me right now. I really don't feel like praying to you at all. But then again, maybe it's that I'm afraid to say what I am going to say. All my life I've carefully chosen my words when I prayed. I wanted to impress you with my sincerity and goodness. But today I'm very angry, the angriest I've ever been at you. You know how much I have wanted a baby. I've prayed the baby would be born healthy. Well God, he's blind. He's blind. How can I ever again believe you're a loving God? What infuriates me more is that my neighbor, an atheist, has four strapping kids. It isn't fair, God. I do blame you for this loss.

We need to give God our grief anger. In the Old Testament, Job, upon loss of his family in a violent storm, hurled anger at God. God understood. The Bible says, "Grieve but grieve with hope." We *do* blame God for some of our losses. We should not feel guilty telling him we are angry.

Is it wise to comfort with "It was God's will?"

I have always held to the belief that the grandest human gift is common sense, knowing when to talk and when to remain silent. Wisdom is not the same as knowledge.

Knowledge consists of what we know, wisdom is what we do with what we know. Educated people are not always wise. They have acquired a wealth of information, but they may lack the wisdom to apply it so as to most benefit others and themselves.

Consider a family in which the youngest child is killed by a drunk driver whose car runs up on the sidewalk. Does one comfort parents with "It is God's will?" Such consolation, though offered with sincerity, tends to minimize (if not completely overlook) the griever's feelings, causing him to wonder, "If this loss is God's will, what right do I have to grieve?" Because we think God wants us to feel joyful, we strive to deny what we really feel.

Asked to explain the Will of God, I respond by saying that, at least for me, God is aware of everything that has happened and will happen to me, though he does not necessarily approve or disapprove of all he knows. God may foresee that next month I will incur a severe burn, but he does not approve of this event. God never takes away our right to choose, and sometimes our choices end in severe losses. If all that happened to us was predetermined, it would take away our incentive to choose.

A myth about God is that believers are accorded protection from life's cruelest losses, that faith in God is an insurance policy, the feature clause being God's protection from severe blows. Fate, that phantom we invent to escape personal responsibility, is a myth. We live in an ordered world. The permanent things that come to us come through commitment and hard work. If the outcome is perceived to be gain, our reward is satisfaction of a job well done. If it is perceived as loss, we assume full responsibility for it, discovering through grief new things about ourselves, others, and God.

145

12
Grieving and Substance Abuse

One evening, after an exasperating afternoon of store-hopping in quest of a new Easter outfit, one of my daughters said, "I couldn't wait to get home, dish myself up a bowl of ice cream, and pour hot chocolate all over it."

Sound familiar? We have all craved food when frustrated, disappointed, lonely, or grieving. Food—like alcohol, drugs, and nicotine—is an artificial support system whose ingredients give our sagging feelings a boost or quiet jumpy nerves. To illustrate what I mean by an artificial support system look at Billy, a first grader, who alone and bored after school stops at the grocery store to buy a sixteen-ounce soft drink and swigs from it on the way home to give himself a lift. When he gets home and finds everyone gone, Billy proceeds to devour a piece of pecan pie—an additional lift. As in Billy's case, an intake of sugar modifies our feelings, or as one compulsive eater put it, "dulls my senses." It isn't that our feelings go away, but that the rush of sugar into our bloodstream helps keep feelings at a manageable level. The hooker is that the lift is temporary; once the sugar effect wears off, we feel more depressed than before.

Our only authentic support system is people and the love and understanding they give us. But people can't always fulfill our needs, so we experiment with artificial support systems. Most of us snack not to appease true physical hunger but to propel a change in our mood. Our snacking is most frequent when we feel the most frustrated or bored, or when our loneliness and grieving seem intolerable.

Food abuse is on the upswing in America. In the past decade, the overweight population has increased 450 percent. According to the National Council on Obesity, 34 percent of all men and 46 percent of all women are now overweight. In the face of rapid change, food abuse is a popular crutch to assist us in managing our loss feelings.

We use drugs, claims Thomas Russell, drug counselor for Sacramento County, California, for one or a combination of reasons. Every day nearly everyone consumes, in one form or another, a drug or chemical—if not nicotine, coffee, or tea, then an occasional aspirin, alcoholic drink, or over-the-counter drug for allergy relief. All these are artificial support systems designed to calm us down, pep us up, or relieve minor physical discomfort.

Another use of drugs is, of course, for illness. Our doctor prescribes penicillin for strep throat; we take it as directed, and we feel better shortly.

But consider a third use of drugs: experimentation with marijuana, cocaine, or heroin. There are generally two types of drug users. One type indulges in moderate or heavy usage for a time, then tapers off and quits. In this way, these users satisfy their curiosity and have no further need of drugs. But some other drug users, who are unable to tolerate stress, grow dependent upon substances to neutralize inner conflicts. Just as an obese person, grieving self-imposed isolation, eats five or six chocolates to quiet negative feelings about herself, this final group of drug users, unable to tolerate their environment, seek complete escape by shooting heroin in order to "nod" or "cocoon out."

An artificial support system, then, is any substance that modifies our mood. For some people, eating sugar is like mainlining for the heroin addict or drinking for the alcoholic. One woman who eats compulsively to manage all of her feelings told me, "After downing several pieces of cake or a quart of ice cream I lie down, close my eyes, and wait for the sugar to hit my blood. It's like a fix."

When Experimentation Begins

During the first year of life, children learn that food does far more than satisfy hunger; it also helps to make unpleasant feelings more manageable. At fourteen, Monique is a compulsive eater. Her parents are divorced. Mother works the 4:00 P.M.-to-midnight shift, leaving Monique home evenings. Monique is allowed to have her friends drop by but she is not to leave the premises. Bored and grieving loss of a relationship with mother (an authentic support system), Monique turns to snacking as a ritual to help her pass the time. In addition, the sugar content of junk food snacks keeps her grief feelings at a level she can cope with.

Food dependency is common during grief, for as with Monique, we find that sugar and carbohydrates register a calming effect on us. Says one woman, grieving loss of a neighbor friend who moved away, "If I don't snack regularly, my feelings overwhelm me and that's when I want to give up."

Many food abusers trace their dependency to grieving a loss. One reports she "turned to food" six months after her marriage soured, stating, "I really can't put my finger on it, but when it hit me that my marriage would never be the high moment of excitement and passion I fantasized, I began grieving silently and salved my feelings with food."

Another woman, whose husband was having an affair, began snacking on candy between meals and got hooked on sugar. Divorce backlash—a child running away from one home to the parent in another home—caused another woman to become hooked on food. She said, "When Jolle ran away to her father's place, I concluded I had failed as a mother. Sweets did wonders to take the edge off my guilt."

A classical example is Norene, at age thirty-five, a whopping 260 pounds and a food addict since the age of six, when her parents separated. She remembers climbing aboard an airplane with mother and looking back at daddy "standing in the terminal crying." Angry at mother for whisking her away with no explanation and wondering if she had done something to cause the breakup, she grieved quietly. Mother ignored her loss questions and feelings, thus depriving Norene of her only genuine support system to work through grief. Her alternative? Food and mounting sugar addiction. This incident took place many years ago, but her conditioned response to any loss since then has been to eat.

Not everyone, of course, eats to make loss feelings manageable. Some of us employ food, drugs, or alcohol as a *reward* for personal gains. A good many people I treat for obesity recollect that as children they were given food by parents either as a reward for good grades in school or as a comforter after treatment of a cut or bruise. "Candy will make the hurt feel better," parents said, or, "Candy will take the pain away." Sometimes sugar was the reward for taking foul-tasting medicine; as it says in the song, "A spoonful of sugar makes the medicine go down." These same children, upon attaining adulthood, continue the same reward system for loss and gains, treating the entire office staff to a steak dinner and drinks upon a job promotion, or if grieving a loss, eating half a chocolate cake in one sitting. "My son celebrates like I do," a member of Overeaters Anonymous told me. "When he graduated from medical school, he took ten of his classmates out to dinner."

Upon a decision to lessen our dependence upon food as an artificial support system, the ritual of snacking must be replaced with another activity. Think about the ritual of snacking. Deciding what to eat, preparing it, chewing, and swallowing all consume time. The eating ritual helps us to pass time and to "space out" feelings by taking the edge off of them for a short while. The food does not drive the feeling out—merely "flattens it out," making it more tolerable.

Or think of the steps within the smoking ritual. Fumbling for the package in our pocket or purse, extracting the cigarette, lighting up, inhaling, exhaling, watching the smoke curl up, and flicking off the ashes takes ten to twelve minutes. Concentrating on the ritual relaxes us and inhaling flattens out our feelings. Chain-smoking, a ritual of many grieving people, spaces our grief feelings but does not dissipate them. Too many people, however, swear to quit smoking and then replace it with snacking.

Some food addicts tell me that once they decided to quit overeating they used tape recorders to record their feelings. Then they either play them back or put the tape on the shelf, most often the latter. Releasing their pent-up feelings was all that was necessary.

Other new activities reported were as follows: "Buying myself a new pair of shoes or anything to make me feel pretty." "Buying an item I would never otherwise buy, like good cologne or subscribing to a magazine." "Just 'spending money.'" "Now, instead of eating spoonfuls of sugar to help manage my feelings, I treat myself to a good friend instead," said a woman, "or go for a walk with her to talk about my feelings."

When I counsel grievers who are abusing food, I often ask them to keep a written log of their feelings each time they are tempted to snack. In so doing, they see the correlation between grief and the activity of eating. Once aware of this relationship, they can choose more responsible ways of handling grief feelings.

Offering hope to food abusers are "loss" organizations such as T.O.P.s (Take Off Pounds) and Overeaters Anonymous. These are authentic support groups designed to provide the food abuser with three things: information, validation, and confrontation. Loss groups strive to show that *misery is optional.* "Because I have always been so dependent upon my husband, whenever he left town on an overnight business trip I ate compulsively to manage my loss feelings," a woman told me. "O.A. supplied me with simple information on better ways to manage my loss feelings, calling another O.A. member to talk of my feelings, for one thing."

These organizations also validate feelings through understanding and acceptance from others "who have the same problem I do." Often, what food abusers most need is hearing the feelings of other overeaters, leading to the revelation that "I am not alone or odd." Excessive weight is a handicap, but even worse (and exhausting) is carrying a stigma of pity and repulsiveness. One obese woman expressed it in these words: "All of my social contacts revolve around ways of trying to help me lose weight. I'm always reminded of my condition and of how repulsive I must be to others." She needed contact with one of the weight-loss organizations to give her unconditional acceptance.

Loss organizations offer unconditional acceptance of grief feelings over not just loss of body figure but a host of other losses. Here is one overweight woman reflecting on hers. "Most of all I grieve the things I want to do but cannot. I like bike riding, but I'm embarrassed about my huge rump. I'd love to swim but I'd feel foolish in a bathing suit. A suntan would be great but someone might look over the fence and laugh at what they see. When I go to a movie, I can't squeeze into a seat. If I went to school, I'd be the fattest person there." Has she ever gone to a party? "I went once but was so terrified someone might ask me to dance I left early."

Alcohol as a Support System

Like sugar, nicotine, caffeine, marijuana, and harder drugs, alcohol is an artificial support system consumed to suppress or release inner feelings. We may simply want to relax after a grueling day, but if we *need* to drink to relax every evening (at noontime or even in the morning) our dependency on alcohol increases and it becomes a crutch. Consider someone grieving, for instance, who, rather than express anger over a loss, drinks instead to numb the feeling. Or, on the opposite side of the coin, the griever might drink to get up the courage to display his anger. The few occasions Lea, one of my grieving clients, shows feelings over loss of her fiance in Viet Nam is when she comes to my office slightly intoxicated. Then she cries over his death or discharges her anger at being "abandoned." Lea knows intellectually that her fiance didn't choose to die and abandon her, but she *feels* angry that her dreams of marriage upon his return were dashed.

Alcohol abuse is anchored in our need for an artificial support system. Unable or unwilling to make necessary decisions or express feelings, we drink to anesthetize ourselves. Mark, a recovered alcoholic, formerly the president of a large manufacturing firm and at present a counselor in a hospital for alcoholics, says his drift into alcoholism was due to a fear of offending anyone and of trying to be a "nice guy." "Alcohol gave me the *courage* to collect bad debts, enforce decisions that might offend people, show anger," he says. For the alcoholic who admits helplessness, the first step back to recovery is often joining a support group like Alcoholics Anonymous.

Drug Abuse and Conditional Belonging

For teen-agers who are struggling for independence from parents but are as yet unsure of a personal identity, drugs offer an opportunity for *conditional belonging* with peers. Users have a common language based on drug-related adventures: how to get drugs, who is taking which drug, things to do when stoned. Drugs give us a set of conditional acquaintances, for the relationships are "iffy"—only *if* we conform are we accepted, only *if* we adopt the values and jargon of fellow users are we valued. So then, if we swear off drugs, we lose our common ground and acquaintances fall away. Peer pressure to conform in order to be accepted is intense among youth.

To lessen our dependence upon drugs as an artificial support system, we will, as with giving up any substance, have to decide on new activities *and new friends*. Drug users are often intense people, for hustling and conning require bustling activity. Therefore, intense activities such as sky-diving, hang-gliding, and rafting—"life-betting activities"— are often good substitutes. In case of less intense people, hiking and athletic games are often undertaken. Are all substances bad? Of itself, nothing is bad or good. It is what we choose to make of them.

Some legitimate drugs are, of course, wonderful. They cure infection and alleviate minor physical discomfort. There is no absolute guideline to determine the point where we are abusing drugs. A friend of mine says that all drugs, including the so-called wonder drugs, should be outlawed, but that is too absolute. Most of us say our yardstick for consuming substances is "moderation" but even that is not an absolute. Three drinks, moderation for one person, may get another person drunk. Guidelines for substance use are individual.

The question to ask ourselves is, are we growing *more*

dependent upon substances to manage our feelings and moods? How we answer that question has a large bearing not only upon our physical health but upon our chosen lifestyle. Perhaps we are working too hard to make ends meet and need substances to relax our jangled nerves, or we may be growing dependent upon substances to give us courage to say and do what we otherwise wouldn't. The thing to remember is that substances do not push our feelings out, they flatten them out. When the effect of the substance has worn off, the feeling comes right back. Substances have not helped us solve anything, they have temporarily made the "problem" more manageable.

Epilogue

Grieving is basically mourning the lost parts of ourselves we invested in the person, place, or object we have lost. Tom had invested twenty years of time and energy in his job. When he was laid off from that job, he grieved the loss of that long investment.

Even people who long to free themselves from unhappy or uncomfortable situations don't take action for fear of losing parts of themselves. Many couples who should separate because they have lost trust in each other and lack motivation to work at the marriage, stay together rather than lose the time and energy they have invested in each other. Divorce, they reason, would be "tossing away" their commitment of time and energy. So they stick out the marriage and go on being miserable.

Every once in a while two people marry who shouldn't marry, but they have given so much of themselves to the other they cannot go their separate ways. Take Joelle and Ed as an example. They were sweethearts all through high school and college. Over those seven years, Joelle permitted Ed to make most of the decisions. But then, during her senior year in college, Joelle began to assert herself more and toyed with the idea of breaking up with Ed. "But I couldn't," she said, "the thought of losing those seven years panicked me. It would be such a waste." They were married. Joelle is sorry now but has strong feelings against divorce. They are "making the most of it," but are unhappy.

The prospect of losing sizable parts of ourselves in others prevents some losses. We decide against the change or the loss, at least for now, feeling we could not endure the grief.

It isn't until a loss occurs that we are made aware of the many parts of ourselves we have invested. And the larger our investment, the more intensely we grieve the loss of our parts. "I feel completely lost," we mourn after separation from a love. We mean, of course, the familiar target of our affection is gone. But, in addition, we truly do mourn our lost parts.

I spent every boyhood summer at a lake in northern Minnesota where I grew fond of a woman by the name of Dovey Lien. I remember her patience as she sat on a high stool behind the candy case, waiting for me to pick two or three cents' worth. In the evenings, sometimes, we sat together on the bench outside the store, she reading the newspaper or waving to the farmers driving by and I eating an ice cream cone. The store itself wasn't much. The weathered exterior was never painted, and the roof sagged pitifully. Workmen tore the dilapidated old place down recently, and I grieved loss of the parts of me (my time, my affection) I'd invested there over forty years.

What Grief Requires of Us

We do not emerge from a grief experience the same person we were before. Grief requires we do *something* about ourselves. Pretending the loss didn't happen only invites trouble, for the grief feelings continue to gnaw away inside of us.

If we have not revealed our feelings to anyone in the past, we begin by taking *little risks* with someone we trust most. If they value our feelings, we can learn to value them too. Others do not know the feeling side of us, so it will take a while for them to adjust to the change. Some may not be able to accept this change in us, however, for our feelings frighten or threaten them. If that is the case, we ought not to be offended. Their fear of feelings is something they will have to work out for themselves.

If at first giving our feelings to a person is too risky, we can start by writing them down or taping them. A tape recorder is safe, for it does not misunderstand us. The important thing is getting our feelings out.

We deny grief feelings because we do not trust them. We fear losing control of ourselves, of harming someone. A client, Marshall, recalls that during a high school basketball game in which he played center, he got so infuriated at the referee that he knocked him cold with a haymaker punch. The story, of course, was juicy fare for the small-town newspaper, and he was razzed mercilessly by everyone. After that unfortunate incident, Marshall decided he'd never trust his anger again for next time, he reasoned, he might go berserk and kill someone. That was many years

159

ago. Today he grieves the loss of an arm in an industrial accident, but he is locked in the anger stage of grief because his anger remains frozen inside of him. He talks of the loss with a clenched fist and set jaw, but only once or twice has he raised his voice. If and when he decides to release that feeling, it will have to be a little bit at a time with someone he trusts.

We must also do something about our deprivation feelings—our emotional, spiritual, intellectual, physical, and sexual needs. Our loneliness demands a new plan for pastimes. Pastiming is the "small talk" we engage in to pass the time. Some people enjoy small talk such as "How have you been?" "Where did you go over the weekend?" Others say it is a waste of time. Some lonely people pore through magazines or take trips in order to gather information to talk about at social gatherings. Small talk, however superficial, is often a prelude to intimacy and the fulfillment of our deprivation needs.

In addition to working on new pastimes, we can set up new rituals. We all develop rituals with persons and pets. Walking the dog each evening is an example. The dog knows the route, and we follow along behind, pausing to chat with neighbors or just enjoy the evening air. If the dog is killed, the loss requires we devise a new ritual to put us back in touch with people. One man, after his divorce, decided that rather than eat breakfast at home (a ritual shared with his wife over eighteen years) he would walk to the corner restaurant each morning. There he struck up new acquaintances. Whatever our loss, the old rituals must be replaced with new ones.

As a supplement to pastimes and rituals, finding a job outside of the home is an option many grievers choose.

And, although merely being with people does not fulfill our needs, we are at least exposing ourselves to that possibility.

We must form a positive attitude toward the *struggle* itself. Unless we choose to find value within the grieving process, our single passion is the *goal* of putting grief behind us quickly. One of the clearest statements on the merit of struggle is made by Hamilton Wright Mabie:

> Every man ought to get character out of his work, even more richly than he gets material reward. The chief value of a great and prolonged struggle is oftener in the effort than in the achievement. The great charm of scholarship is in the scholar and not in his acquirement. The noblest outcome of a great business career is not the fortune which rewards it, but the mastery of affairs which it develops in the merchant and financier. Character is a permanent possession. It can never be taken from us.[1]

The same principle holds true for grief. We are meant to get *character* out of the struggle.

Finally, we must reexamine our commitments. Are they demanding the best of us today? If not, perhaps they need updating.

We do not know the value of long-standing commitments or priorities until their loss is threatened. Often we discover that those things we are certain we cannot survive without, we can really do without quite easily. Loss of money is a good example. Most of us cannot conceive of functioning

1. Hamilton Wright Mabie, *Works and Days* (New York: Dodd, Mead, 1899), p. 196.

without money beyond one day. A friend of mine who was traveling in Italy lost his wallet and $200. At first he panicked, thinking, "I'm stuck. I can't do a thing now." But rather than act upon the paralyzing first impulse by writing home for money, he decided to wait and try an experiment; he would sleep under the stars, hitchhike, and work for his meals along the way. And so he took back roads, walked through small towns, and got acquainted with average citizens, gaining insight into a part of the culture most citizens never see. In addition, he learned about the generosity of people. But most important he amazed himself—he could survive without money for one week.

We often say, "I couldn't go on if Jill left me," or, "I'd fold up if I lost that investment." But whatever our commitment, we need to be prepared to release it at any time. No relationship is permanent. Because our values change, so our commitments need updating.

Frank, a real estate agent, decided one year that his top priority was to earn $50,000 in sales commissions. He earned that sum but paid dearly with a heart attack. Grieving that loss, Frank decided that time spent with his family and two children was a higher priority than time devoted to gathering his fortune. Frank, then, chose to make of grief a gift, for he saw it as opportunity for reevaluating his priorities.

One of the most dramatic examples I have ever seen of grief as a gift is Debbie. She is forty-five, works as a teacher, and has two sons in high school. After nineteen years of a "comfortable" marriage, her husband left her for another woman. Since she had no inkling he was courting someone else, that fact alone shocked Debbie. But she had been raised in a strongly religious home in which divorce was looked upon as an unforgivable sin. She had always considered herself to be immune from this worst of all losses. After her husband left, she slept but three or four hours a night and lost fifteen pounds. When the numbness of shock began wearing off, she cried—softly at first, then breaking into sobs. She went through every stage of the grief cycle, but guilt over what God and her church friends would think of her now gave her the most trouble. In addition, she felt guilty over failing as a wife. At first she thought of everything wrong she had done, thus assuming all responsibility for the loss. Thinking back to her first weeks of grief, she recalls, "In the teachers' lounge I talked of the divorce with anyone who would listen, the janitor included. People got so sick of it they began avoiding me. That did it. I knew it was time to get professional help."

She did. Her first bit of insight was, "I'd handled every loss up to this point in my life, but I can't handle divorce." She had to admit helplessness. The point of helplessness, however, was an opportunity, for it demanded she *choose* between despairing or drawing on previously untapped resources within herself.

One of the most interesting things in life is the unexpected development of qualities which sometimes takes place in people who have shown little or no promise of exceptional talent or ability.

This development is sometimes as great a surprise to the man in whom it takes place as to his friends. He awakens to find himself in possession of a force, the presence of which he did not suspect. Very few men completely unfold all that is in them. As the earth is full of treasures of all kinds, the existence of which is not suspected in many localities, and which are presently to bring private fortunes to these localities, so there are men and women in the world over who are rich in power of the highest kind, but who have no suspicion of that fact because they have never given themselves full development through activity.[2]

The newspaper recently carried a syndicated story of the heroic feat of a sixteen-year-old-boy. While his father was working under the car, it slipped off its jack, pinning him to the ground. The boy, looking on, rushed over and lifted the car by the back bumper far enough off the ground to enable rescuers to pull his father out. Of his Herculean feat the amazed teen-ager commented, "I didn't think I had it in me."

Drawing upon what we didn't think we had in us is exciting. Our severe losses may pull us down to the point of feeling totally helpless. But if we, like this teen-ager, choose to find opportunity in helplessness and test our old limits of strength (or patience, etc.), we are often amazed at our unused power.

Debbie was. Prior to her divorce, all of her friendships revolved around the church. She had, in her own words, "fallen into a horrible rut where I related only to people like me, who thought and felt like I did." After her divorce, she decided to risk new friendships. People's response amazed her. "If I walked into a new place and initiated conversa-

2. Ibid, p. 65.

tions with people I've never met, their response was usually warm."

But Debbie talks of other gains too, stating that if she marries again she will "work at love." "My marriage seemed so secure I thought I could just coast along," she says remorsefully. "I took my husband for granted the last ten years of our marriage."

It may require the loss of a relationship to teach us that love is indeed hard work.

This matter of going the "second mile" with people is faithfulness in remembering the little things of love. A husband I know makes it a point of opening the garage door for his wife on rainy nights, thus sparing her the nuisance of that little task. Or there is the mother who folds the sheet and blanket back on her teen-age daughter's bed so that when her daughter gets home late from a baby-sitting job she can slip right into bed. That her mother *thought* of this warms her daughter's heart.

In my files are gifts my daughters gave me when they were little. Gifts like grass and dandelions pasted to newspaper or wilted weeds in an envelope. In terms of dollars and cents these things are worth nothing, but I treasure them because they symbolize being remembered. The value of any gift is not its monetary value but that a friend remembered us.

It is important to remember friends and family *now*. Debbie discovered through her grief. Losing her husband focused all of the things they talked of doing down through the years but postponed, saying, "There's always time later on." That time, however, "never rolled around."

Why do we always dream of having more time in the

future, telling ourselves today that we have but a spare five minutes here or twenty minutes there, and what can we do in those fragments of time? Next week we'll get to them, we say, or next year. When our responsibilities are fewer, we'll have time to read the new books or study the languages we need to learn. But those moments never come. We must do those things in the *odds* and *ends* of time each day. There is no future outside of us; it lies within us, and we make it for ourselves. Rarely do we have large blocks of time in which, uninterrupted, we can start and complete a task. And so novels are read on the bus to and from work or paintings are dabbled at in bits of time evenings. *Life is now.*

Debbie eventually came to ralize that her marriage years were not wasted. In fact, she decided if she could do it over again, she would marry the same man. "I did the best I could with what I knew then," she says wisely. Grieving the loss of a love, we are tempted to think the years together were a waste and wonder how we ever tolerated what we did? But the point is we did tolerate it, and we did try to make the most of it with the resources that were available to us. There's no use to flagellate ourselves with guilt over failure or anger over waste.

I once read that an old-time Oriental army carried with it every sort of convenience and luxury, hindering quick movement; a modern army discards everything but the weapons necessary for the battle. There is genius in knowing what to remember and what to leave behind. No experience is wasted providing we learn something through it. The past is only valuable for what we can learn from it.

Debbie does not blame God for her loss, but at first she prayed God would reconcile them. Then the thought struck her she was asking God to give her what she wanted. She was not praying—she was begging. She changed her prayers from begging to simply talking with God, asking him to help her through the crisis.

I like the example of Debbie because she chose to make grief into a positive experience—a process working for her instead of against her. Today, looking back on her grief, she says, "Right after the loss I didn't think I could make it. I thought that if I could just survive, it would be a miracle. Then I began to see some of the possibilities for my own personal growth through grief. I chose to think of the process as a gift and not something to get behind me as quickly as possible."

We, like Debbie, can choose to make grief a gift. Within every loss there are seeds for gain and new beginnings. The worth of grieving lies within the struggle itself. There is no absolute way to make the most of the process. Each of us explores and decides what choices to risk, and then we assume responsibility for the consequences of our choices. That is the opportunity, the challenge, of grief.